The Craft of the Fireman

The Craft of the Fireman

Trevor Matthews

First published in 2020

British Library Cataloguing in Publication Data

A catalogue record for this book is available from the British Library.

ISBN 978 1 85794 567 6

Silver Link Books
Mortons Media Group Limited
Media Centre
Morton Way
Horncastle
LN9 6JR
Tel/Fax: 01507 529535

email: sohara@mortons.co.uk
Website: www.nostalgiacollection.com

Printed and bound in the Czech Republic

Note: For simplicity, 'fireman' is referred to as a male role in this book, but it is acknowledged that there are now many female 'firemen' at work on heritage railways.

Title page: A fireman on the footplate of GWR pannier tank No 7714. The damper levers can be seen immediately under the fireman's shovel, with the back damper on the third notch. *Tim Thursfield courtesy Express and Star*

Contents

Trevor Matthews in his pit gear with Cannock Chase Coalfields' last steam locomotive, No 7, standing outside the locomotive workshop at Littleton in 1974. *Jack Muddell/Express and Star*

Foreword by David C. Williams
Chairman, Severn Valley Railway Company

The efficient burning of coal has always been of great importance to steam locomotive operators, and today, because of the reduced availability of good steam coals causing ever rising prices, it is even more important than it was between 2010 and 2012, the years during which this book was written.

The author, Trevor Matthews, was a colleague of mine on the Board of Severn Valley Railway Holdings plc from 1975 until 1992, and indeed is an expert on this subject. He joined the coal mining industry in 1951, and used his knowledge and experience to source good-quality steam coal for the railway. This was initially Park Hards from West Cannock No 5 Colliery until the district producing it unfortunately had to be sealed off due to inunedation, to be followed by Warwickshire Thick Coal from Newdigate Colliery and, when this closed, the same seam from Daw Mill.

The objective of this work is to motivate locomotive firemen to endeavour to improve their performance on each successive firing turn, so suggestions are made as to how this can be achieved.

The benefits of good firing, together with good driving, were demonstrated in May 1990 when Trevor, driving BR 4-6-0 No 75069 with Don Dutton firing, completed a full mid-week's SVR services, comprising 325 train miles with 100 booked stops, without needing to take coal. This achievement was recognised in the Autumn 1990 edition of *SVR News*, when the Bridgnorth Shedmaster, John Robinson, exhorted other footplate crews to try to emulate this, thus improving efficiency and significantly reducing costs.

I have no hesitation in recommending this eminently practical book covering a subject vital to heritage railway preservation.

An essential introduction

Dear reader, have you ever seen a booklet beginning with 'An Essential Introduction'? No! Neither have I, but if you read on it will become clear to you why it is essential. *The Craft of the Fireman* was never intended to appear in book form as the original objective was to write a series of articles for a small annual magazine published by a society and specifically addressed to the members of that society, so please read on. Lest anyone should think I considered myself an authority on the firing of steam locomotives when I hung up my shovel in June 1979 on being promoted to driver, I must inform them that the idea

Trevor Matthews

of ever writing anything about it never entered my head for around 28 years, and even then it was introduced by another person.

That person was Mary McCullough, who was the secretary of the Vintage Trains Society and also the editor of bi-annual newsletters together with a small annual magazine. Although I knew her by sight, I had never spoken to her until the 1 July 2006, when we happened to be standing next to each other on Platform 12 at Crewe watching No 4936 *Kinlet Hall* being watered on a trip to Holyhead.

For some unknown reason the conversation turned to the firing of steam locomotives, in which she appeared to be quite interested. At this time Vintage Trains was running steam-hauled trains in double figures per annum (excluding the 'Shakespeares') and, as I was a regular passenger and Mary a regular steward, our paths crossed quite often. After our original conversation she made a habit of having a chat with me about firing on each occasion.

After about 18 months she asked me if I would consider writing something on the subject for the VTS publication 'Steam in Trust'. I politely declined, on the grounds that Vintage Trains had two experienced main-line firemen in Alastair Meanley and Dean Morris and I did not wish to step on anyone's toes.

Nevertheless, our conversations continued and from time to time she would attempt to persuade me to change my mind, although never pressurising me to do so. Her argument was always that I should make the benefit of my experience available to others, and it would be a shame if it was to be lost. After another couple of years, in a moment of weakness in December 2009, and knowing that I could write plenty, I agreed to do so without having considered what I was going to write.

I did, however, impose two conditions, the most important of which was that she would provide an introduction stating that she had asked me to write the article, to which she agreed.

As soon as I gave it some thought I realised that I had undertaken a considerable task. The readership was going to be people interested in steam locomotives and travelling behind them, but with little knowledge of footplate fittings and operation. I am of the opinion that the work of the steam locomotive fireman has always been grossly undervalued, so if I was to write about it I would have to demonstrate what a skilled occupation it is, even to perform it reasonably efficiently. This obviously meant starting from scratch.

Things went according to plan and the first part appeared in the 2010 edition of 'Steam in Trust'. However, it had become increasingly obvious that the whole work would be much too long to be covered solely in the magazine, so extra pages were incorporated in the newsletters in 2011. Even then, what I had already written would have taken too long to cover in their publications.

As it happens, it all came to halt in 2012 when Vintage Trains took over the editorship and at the time decided to discontinue the articles, although they had been very well received. I had by this time got so far in front of the published parts that I decided to finish it anyway, which I did towards the end of 2012.

So, what was I going to do, if anything, with it? After giving it much thought I decided to obtain an opinion, if possible, from an expert on footplate work, and who better to seek one from than the renowned R. H. N. (Dick) Hardy? Accordingly I phoned him in around March 2013, told him what I had done and asked him if he would like to read it. He said he would, so I mailed him a draft.

A few weeks elapsed before he phoned me back to tell me he considered it worthy of publication, but he wanted to study it in more detail and take notes. This would take some time because he was exceptionally busy. I spoke to him again a few months later and we discussed the possibility of it being published in a railway magazine.

Eventually I received a letter from him dated 25 May 2014, which started, 'Dear Trevor, At last! I have been through your work-of-art a second time and I have learned about various things that I have never considered.' You can imagine how gratified I was to read that coming from such an authority on footplate work. He continued with, '…it is very interesting, knowledgeable and unusual, which is good.'

I concluded that he regarded it as unusual because, like myself, he had never before read anything on firing that started with the chemistry of combustion and went right through to main-line work, and neither had I. He also offered to write to a prospective editor to '…see if I can get him to accept it in principle', but did warn that '…he may say that it is too long and will take up too much room, even over a period.'

He did appear to be fairly sure, however, that it would be published in some form or another by stating, 'There will be old timers like myself or, more important, old timers amongst the drivers and firemen … who will be fascinated!!'

Consequently, I did offer it to a magazine and his prediction came true. They were prepared to do it in e-book form but, as I still live in the age of steam, this form is not 'real' to me, so I declined the offer and, for one reason or another, it lay dormant again until July 2016.

I then decided that it would be a waste not to continue, but with the prolific publishers of the 1970s and '80s on steam locomotive footplate work having disappeared, I had it e-mailed to another publisher of works on railway subjects, albeit not locomotive work. They were interested enough to print a copy of it, so that they could examine it in more detail, and were quite impressed by it but decided that it was too far removed from their normal spheres of activity to publish. They were kind enough, however, to send me a nice letter and a printed copy.

Again, I allowed it to lie dormant and, although there have been mitigating circumstances, I am ashamed to say that it was only the sad death of Dick Hardy earlier this year that has finally, over five years since writing was completed, spurred me into more vigorous action. I feel that because of his interest, encouragement and time spent on the project, I would be letting him down if there was no end product.

So, if you find the following interesting, informative and possibly even enjoyable, you must give a great deal of credit to Mary McCullough for her interest, gentle persuasion and tenacity over a period of 3½ years, and Dick Hardy for his interest in the writings of an amateur footplateman and his encouragement and support in order to get it into print.

Without both of them you would not have had the opportunity to do so.

Trevor Matthews C.Eng., B.Eng., M.I.Min.E.
August 2018

Acknowledgements

I would like to thank Steve Matthews for editing the draft; Alison Marsh, Steve Matthews and Mary McCullough for typing, Phil Matthews and Steve Matthews for photographs of footplate and tools; and Mick Lucas for the illustration of the cross section of a firebox.

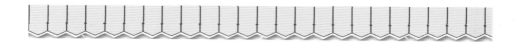

The importance of the fireman

Those who have been on a footplate experience course, been given a short talk on firing and shown how to use an injector, provided they can stand on a footplate and have minimal skill with a shovel, know that they can generate enough steam to get a lightweight train (generally one coach) from A to B. However, this is vastly different from having to provide steam at or near the registered pressure of the boiler and at such a rate that the engine can develop the horsepower needed to produce the sort of main-line running that we are extremely fortunate to be able to experience at the present time.

A driver is still a driver whatever sort of motive power is in use, but the fireman, given a grate, a vessel in which to boil water and a supply of coal and water, is analogous to the engine in a diesel locomotive inasmuch that he is the sole provider of power. No matter how good a driver may be, he cannot produce a top performance unless his fireman does so, and whilst drivers tend to get the credit they also recognise that it is essentially a team effort. As C. Hamilton Ellis once said, 'A good journey by steam is a realised work of art.'

In the hey-day of steam many millions of tons of coal were burnt annually by the railway companies, so any small improvement in the thermal efficiency of the locomotives could have a significant effect on the balance sheet. To this end, locomotive engineers tried a number of innovations over the years, most of which were abandoned on the grounds of additional costs of construction and maintenance. Probably not many people are aware that the biggest improvement could have been effected if the overall standards of firing had been brought nearer those of the best firemen.

Footplate observations in steam days showed that some firemen used twice as much coal as the best firemen on the same duty. As a corollary to Hamilton Ellis's comment, top firemanship is an art in itself; I will attempt to explain why.

• 2 •
The chemistry of combustion

To realise the complexity of a fireman's task if top performance with efficiency is to be achieved, it is necessary to understand the basic composition of coal, which, for the sake of simplicity, may be considered as two main constituents: volatile matter and fixed carbon. Maximum efficiency requires the fireman to achieve complete combustion as nearly as possible. For example, 1lb (0.454kg) of carbon completely burned to carbon dioxide (CO_2) produces 14,550 British Thermal Units (BThUs) or 15,348 kilojoules (kj) of heat whereas, if only burned to carbon monoxide (CO), this is reduced to 4,350 BThUs (4,580kj) i.e. about 70% of the potential heat value is wasted. Likewise with the volatile matter content of the coal.

Low volatile coals such as Welsh dry steam coals (volatile matter in the range 14% to 20%) are in short supply and most locomotive coals used today are high volatile with a volatile matter percentage around 30%-35% or even higher.

This contains nearly all the hydrogen present in the fuel, and since hydrogen has a weight-for-weight heating value about four times that of carbon (1lb or 0.454 kg being completely burned to water vapour, providing 62,100 BThUs or 65,506 kj of heat), it is obvious that failure to burn the hot gases being discharged from the firebed known as hydrocarbons, and resulting in black smoke (the 'clag' so beloved by some photographers), is a major cause of excessive coal consumption.

The grate on a steam locomotive works on the same principle as any other solid fuel grate. The firebed is supported on bars with gaps between them to allow air, which contains 21% oxygen by volume, to permeate the firebed from below. A means of adjusting this air, known as primary air, is needed in order to assist in controlling the rate of burning, and adequate provision must be made for accommodating the ash resulting from combustion without interfering with the flow of the primary air. Finally, and most importantly, is a means of mixing sufficient secondary air, admitted through the firehole, with the hydrocarbons in order to enhance combustion of this portion of the coal constituents, which has the highest calorific value.

So what features are provided on a steam locomotive in order for the fireman to carry out his task efficiently? The grate, the area of which is determined by the designed output of the boiler, is formed of individual

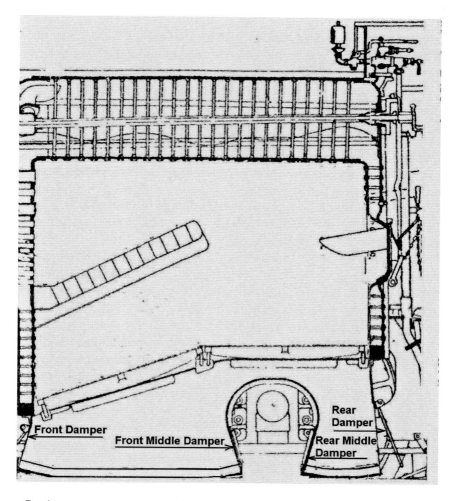

Firebox arrangements on GWR 'Hall' and 'Castle' Class locomotives.
Mick Lucas

	Boiler dimensions:	
	'Hall' No 1 Standard	'Castle' No 8 Standard
Grate area	27.1sq ft	29.4sq ft
	Heating surfaces:	
Firebox	155sq ft	163sq ft
Tubes	1,687sq ft	1,858sq ft
Superheater	263sq ft	263sq ft
Total	2,105sq ft	2,284sq ft

firebars (sections in modern rocking grates), not only for convenience of installation, but so that any that become eroded or damaged by burning can be replaced without having to replace the whole grate. Ash is collected in an ashpan; this also performs the additional function of regulating the primary air supply to the underside of the grate via the damper doors, which also provide access for raking out during disposal (rocking grates are combined with hopper ashpans, which have bottom discharge doors, thus obviating this latter unpleasant job). Needless to say, ashpans must retain any hot embers falling between the firebars and prevent them from dropping onto the track and causing fires, and have a large enough capacity, under normal circumstances, to allow the passage of sufficient primary air. However, by far the most important features regarding the efficiency with which the coal is burned are the brick arch and the firehole deflector plate.

The arch is built from firebricks or concrete and extends from just below the bottom tubes in the tubeplate at the front of the inner firebox, back towards the firehole door, and usually extends over half the length of the grate or slightly more. Its role is to direct the hydrocarbons leaving the firebed back towards the firehole door against the stream of secondary air coming in so as to mix them with the oxygen in that air in order to achieve complete combustion so far as is possible. The mixing is enhanced by the deflector plate, which projects into the firebox from above the firehole door and directs the secondary air slightly downwards against the hot gases coming towards it from under the brick arch. On a long firebox the deflector plate is usually about 18 inches (46cm) in length when new, but shortens in use as a result of burning. In addition to the hydrocarbons, carbon monoxide given off by the fixed carbon burning on the grate has to be converted into carbon dioxide in the interests of efficiency, and since this requires a minimum temperature of 1,210°F (654°C), a very hot fire is absolutely essential.

Despite the effects of the arch and deflector plate, mixing of the hydrocarbons with the secondary air is not perfect and to achieve complete combustion requires 20% more air than the theoretical amount. This is unfortunate because air contains 79% by volume of the inert gas nitrogen, which gets heated to a high temperature before being discharged up the chimney as a total loss. However, the loss from using too much excess air as compared with too little is much less; for example, if only 2.5% excess air is used, the avoidable heat loss is 11.4% compared with only 3.1% for 40% of excess air. The good fireman will therefore always run with a clear chimney in preference to a smoky one!

The fireman exercises control over the boiler by adjusting the depth of the firebed, the amount of opening of the damper(s), the use either of the flap that can be raised to partly cover the firehole or partial opening of the firehole doors to regulate the flow of secondary air, the boiler water level by use of the injectors, and the blower valve. This latter controls small steam jets in the smokebox that create a partial vacuum in order to draw the hot gases from the firebox and discharge them up the chimney when the regulator is closed and there is no exhaust steam passing through the smokebox to do the same job. The blower valve has a number of uses: being just cracked open when the locomotive is stationary and in steam to stop egress of hot gases from the firebox into the cab; to raise steam more quickly from cold when the boiler pressure has started to rise; when building the fire prior to departure; as a means of recovering steam pressure when the regulator is closed out on the road at times when the boiler is suffering from steaming problems; and to prevent blow-backs onto the footplate when entering confined tunnels at speed.

Vintage Trains currently has three types of locomotive with main-line certification, namely pannier tank, 'Hall' and 'Castle'. The pannier has a flat grate of 15.3sq ft (1.42sq m) area, but 'Halls' and 'Castles' both have grates with a flat rear section (about 45% of the grate area) to a point above the trailing coupled axle (see the illustration in Chapter 2), and a section inclined downwards at about 15° from that point to the front of the firebox, with grate areas of 27.1sq ft (2.52sq m) and 29.4sq ft (2.73sq m) respectively. This type of grate is almost universal on 4-6-0 locomotives having a wheel diameter of 6 feet (1.83m) or more, because of the height of the trailing coupled axle above rail level. The ashpan on a pannier has front and rear damper doors, while 'Halls' and 'Castles' generally have two additional dampers, the front middle and rear middle, which are situated in the ashpan either side of the rear coupled axle (see the illustration on page 13). Damper doors are usually operated by inverted L-shaped levers, projecting through slots in a steel section of the footplate. They are notched on their trailing edges to engage with the footplate and thus retain the damper opening set by the fireman. Only one slot is provided on GW engines, with the above type of grate, designed to burn slow-reacting Welsh steam coals and required to quickly accelerate heavy trains up to express speeds.

All three locomotive types mentioned have what is known as narrow fireboxes, which means that the lower part is sited between the main frames of the locomotive. Because of the thickness of the waterwalls of the firebox, which varies slightly in different classes of locomotive, the width of the grate is limited to about 3 feet (0.91m), or just over, and in consequence long grates of the order of 8ft 10in (2.69m) in the case of the 'Halls' and 9ft 8in (2.95m) in 'Castles'.

As can be imagined, grates of this size involve large fires to be managed, for which the fireman is provided with a number of hand tools. In addition to the firing shovel and coal hammer, more of which later, there is also a set of fire-irons that are essential equipment for any locomotive with a conventional grate out on the road, but the fireman hopes that circumstances will not arise that demand their use. The keen fireman will, however, organise things so that he will use one or all of them for his own benefit at one or more strategic points on the journey dependent upon the time available and the condition of the fire.

The minimum set of fire-irons comprises a dart, a bent dart, a pricker or slice, and a clinker shovel, or paddle as it is sometimes called, all of which have a metal shank formed at the handle end into a loop, either circular, triangular, or what can be described as a flattened oval for ease of identification when stored in fire-iron tunnels, all of which also provide a firm grip. The dart is a straight-shanked tool for breaking clinker by means of what I can best describe as a large arrowhead (which quickly gets blunted in use) at the business end of the shank, while the bent dart is much shorter in length, the curved shank enabling clinker to be broken in the back corners and under the firehole and the back corners to be cleaned during disposal. The pricker has a blade some 9 inches (23cm) or so long, fixed at right-angles to the end of the shank and is used for spreading the fire when steam raising, livening the fire up if not burning properly, breaking up the crust that forms above the firebed with caking coals, riddling ashes and small pieces of clinker through the firebars when the fire has been run down in order to check the condition of the grate, and to raise thin pancakes of clinker off the firebars. The clinker shovel requires no explanation other than to say that it must be long enough to reach the front of the grate, as must the pricker; in the case of a 'Castle', this means a length of around 11 feet (3.3m). To have the necessary strength and resistance to heat, such tools, the clinker shovel in particular, are quite heavy. I will deal with their use in more detail later.

When considering the work of the fireman, probably most people in their mind's eye see coal being shovelled through the firehole, so it is worthwhile looking at what this entails. It must be said, however, that this is only part of his overall job of managing the boiler. This is done by means of the depth of the firebed, the damper(s) and the firehole door openings, and the injectors to force feedwater into the boiler to maintain the correct water level as well as to prevent blowing off or, more importantly, to guard against exposing the firebox crown plate, causing the fusible plugs to melt and having to drop the fire. If steaming is a problem, the blower valve may have to be used to raise steam pressure when the regulator is closed. The fireman is also of course required to assist the driver with sightings at all times when he is not occupied with his firing duties.

4

The fireman's environment and firing tools

The location in which the fireman works is bounded by the firebox backplate, the locomotive footplate and, on tender locomotives, the fallplate between the locomotive and tender, the tender footplate and tender front. The fallplate is hinged to the trailing edge of the locomotive footplate and covers the gap between the locomotive and tender footplates, with its trailing edge lying on the tender footplate. On tank engines, the footplate extends to the front of the bunker. The tender itself is unique in the train formation insofar as its weight reduces markedly during the journey; for example, the standard 'Hall' or 'Castle' tender with 6 tons of coal and 4,000 gallons of water weighs 46t 14cwt (47.5 tonnes) full, but only 22t 17cwt (23.26 tonnes), empty. This means that, of necessity, the springing has to be a compromise, with a consequence that on anything less than perfect track the tender can behave very differently between being full and nearly empty. This compounds the fact that the locomotive and tender pitch and roll differently in the first place, and the fallplate partly accommodates this, particularly when split into two halves down the centre line of the locomotive. However, at speed, the movement of the locomotive relative to the tender on poor track can determine how the fireman carries out his task; consequently he may have to restrict his firing actions to locations when he would not normally choose to fire, simply because of the difficulty of getting coal through the firehole door as a result of the violent motions of the locomotive and tender. Locomotive designers were aware of this and, in a number of cases, e.g. BR 'Standards', the footplate was extended as close as possible to the tender front and the fallplate eliminated.

Passengers only used to travelling in bogie coaches may find this difficult to believe, but a 60-foot (18.3m) coach mounted on softly sprung bogies (axle loading only normally 9/10 tons) equalises the track imperfections to give a very smooth ride and is a totally different animal compared with a steam locomotive. This is due to a number of factors such as the much stiffer springing demanded by coupled axle loadings, more than double the above, together with a rigid wheelbase about two-fifths of the length of the locomotive; in a 4-6-0 this is only about two-thirds of the length of a carriage. These alone make the locomotive's ride very inferior to that of a coach.

On top of all this are the heavy vibrations set up by the reciprocating masses of the pistons and crossheads, the combination of reciprocating and rotating forces of the connecting rods, and the centrifugal forces generated by the coupling rods, all of which, although partly balanced, transmit vibrations to the main frames of the locomotive through the coupled wheel axles.

In a 'Hall' Class locomotive travelling at 60mph, the driving wheels rotate at around 4.8 times per second! Since each revolution involves two strokes of the pistons, this means that the heavy masses of the pistons and crossheads have to be accelerated from rest to a very high speed, then brought to rest again almost ten times per second. The stresses imposed are immense and it is not surprising that cracking of locomotive mainframes at the top corners of the hornguides has been a perennial problem, and that a locomotive footplate can be a vibrating, noisy, hot and dusty environment.

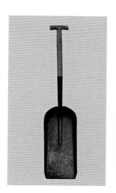

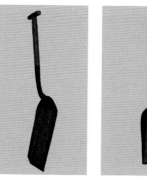

A fireman's pick
The GWR large-bladed shovel
The LMS-type shovel, with a medium-length shank

The dimensions that concern the fireman are typically about 3ft 6in (1.07m) from the firebox backplate to the fallplate hinge, 1ft 2in (35.6cm) for the fallplate, and a further 1ft 9in to 2ft 0in (53-61cm) to the front of the tender coal space, i.e. about 16 feet (4.88m) to the front of the fire grate on a 'Castle' and around another 14 feet (4.27m) to the back of the tender coal space. Probably the most important dimension from the fireman's point of view is the level from which coal has to be lifted, which on these locomotives is footplate level compared with an average of 15 inches (38cm) or so on LMS locomotives, for example, where the bottom of the tender coal space is raised above footplate level to what is known as a 'shovelling plate'.

One can only conclude that crew considerations were of no consequence to the GWR's legendary Chief Mechanical Engineer, George Jackson Churchward, and his successors were afraid to change that which he had decreed!

The other two hand tools are the firing shovel and coal pick. The latter is a dual-purpose tool with a square-headed hammer on one side of the shaft and a pick blade on the other. It was an absolutely essential piece of equipment when all the locomotives on the important services were supplied with large coal of 6 inches (15.2cm) plus, although the Great Western Railway did favour a rather smaller size because of the difficulties of breaking Welsh dry steam coal into a useable size without reducing it to slack, and the need to expose a higher percentage of the coal surface to oxidation in order to enhance the rate of combustion.

The main use of the pick blade these days is for pulling coal forward in the tender, while the hammer can come in useful in dealing with footplate problems from time to time by means of 'gentle persuasion'. However, since running under the wires has been permitted (as a result of which entry into the tender is banned), long wooden-handled rakes have to be used.

Now there are firing shovels and firing shovels, and the GW and LMS types are as different as chalk and cheese.

The GW type is long-bladed and parallel-sided with a capacity reckoned to be 20lb (9.1 kg), which necessitates a short handle, while the LMS type has a much smaller, narrower, tapering pan of about half the capacity and a longer handle with a varying length to give an overall dimension of a maximum of about 3ft 9in (1.14m).

Having been made aware of the parameters of the fireman's sphere of operation, it is worthwhile considering the physical operation of transferring the coal from the tender into the firebox before looking at the types of coal and firing methods required for best performance. Although I had fired on GW tank engines for several years, it was not until 1977 that I had the opportunity to fire on a 'Hall'. A standard GW-type shovel was on the footplate and naturally this was what I used.

By the time I had completed my first firing turn I was convinced that this shovel was by no means the best tool for the job given that the tender had been coaled with high volatile hards.

Having had experience on LMS 'Black Five' and 8F locomotives of very similar dimensions, I found the capacity of the GW shovel unnecessarily large and, together with having to lift the coal from footplate level, this put an additional strain on the back.

Secondly the short handle made it feel unbalanced and, due to its wider blade with raised sides, it was more difficult to drive it at full extent of the right arm into the coal as it got further back in the tender, in addition to the reach of the shovel being less in any case. Quite frankly I felt it was not the best tool for the job and came to the conclusion that it was again a case of GW resistance to change – we've always done it this way so it must be right! Some firemen think it is macho to use such a shovel, and disparagingly call the LM type a 'teaspoon'. Some teaspoon, if it is adequate for the 50sq ft (4.64sq m) grates of the 'Duchesses' which are almost 46% bigger in area than the largest GW grates at 34.3sq ft (3.18sq m) on the 'Kings', excluding, of course, that one-off 41.8sq ft (3.88sq m) of *The Great Bear*, which was itself rebuilt as a 'Castle'.

Consequently, for my next firing term on a 'Hall' I selected a long-handled LMS-type shovel and quickly found it a great improvement. GW locomotives are right-hand drive, so it is natural for the fireman to fire right-handed and, facing the tender with the right foot on or near the fallplate hinge and the left foot nearer the firehole, the loaded shovel could easily be lifted with the left hand placed over, instead of under, the shank of the handle, thus reducing the degree of back bending required. Doing this has the effect of rotating the wrist through 180°, which reverses the grip of the left-hand on the shovel, giving the added bonus that no turning of the body is required for the firing operation – a glance over the left shoulder is all that is needed. The narrower, tapering shovel blade enables coal to be placed very accurately on the firebed and I found no difficulty whatsoever in putting the coal anywhere required other than the back corners, including the front of the box since the firing stance allows a free swing of the shovel. Of course with a hot fire a restriction on the number of shovelsful at any one firing is needed in order to avoid scorched overalls, but this has the benefit of almost ensuring the 'little and often' technique. Also the sides of the shovel, tapering down to zero at the blade tip, make for easier penetration of the coal and, coupled with the long handle, coal much further back in the tender is accessible with this type of shovel. I should imagine that other firemen may have used this technique, although I have never heard it mentioned, but I am certain no one will have tried it with a GW-type shovel. It could be described as sacrilege to use this bludgeon on such a thoroughbred as a 'Castle' burning high volatile coal, where a rapier would be much more appropriate.

Having said that, there were valid reasons for using a large-capacity shovel with the low volatile coals that the Great Western engines were designed to burn, despite the lower consumption resulting from the (normally) higher calorific value, as will become apparent when firing methods are discussed.

Tender design

Before leaving the physical task of transferring coal from the tender to the firebox, there is another aspect to be looked at, and that is the tender coal space. Anything that assists in delivering the coal to the point where it can be accessed by the fireman's shovel is clearly desirable, so the greater the height to which coal can be accommodated at the front of the tender the better, and this, together with the inclination of the sides of the coal bunker combined with the oscillations of the tender, determine the extent to which a tender is self-trimming, i.e. it delivers coal to the point of shovelling.

Those who have looked at the tender front of *Princess Elizabeth* or *Kolhapur*, for example, will have seen that it matches the profile of the cab roof, which means that the tender can be filled to the maximum of the loading gauge so that, even when a couple of tons have been used, the depth of coal in the tender combined with the angle of repose of the coal and the oscillations of the tender still feed coal towards the fireman's shovel. LMS Stanier tenders cannot be improved upon in this respect.

The standard Great Western tenders on the other hand, because of the much lower height of the coal space, quickly run out of any self-trimming effect and also have a horizontal ledge a foot or more wide running round the coal space from which coal has to be pulled, so the physical effort involved in transferring the coal from the tender to the firebox is correspondingly greater.

On the other hand, the access to the tender coal space through the doors is much

A Stanier tender front, showing the shovelling plate above footplate level, and the door flaps easier on the Great Western example when coal further back needs to be pulled forward, a feature that is much appreciated when it comes to disposal in steam of a locomotive with a long standard fixed grate. The Hawksworth tender as fitted to No 5043 has some of the benefits of the Stanier tender but again does not maximise the potential height of the coal space.

All tenders have an opening under the doors to allow access to the coal,

but if the coal is of a small size the oscillations of the tender when full can cause the footplate to flood with coal. Some of the Stanier tenders are fitted with hinged flaps at the bottoms of the doors to control this. However, with any type of tender a fireman will always rig up a board or two to reduce the size of the orifice, if necessary, because one of his responsibilities is to keep the footplate tidy and it is not unknown for broken ankles to have resulted from cobbles of coal lying around on the footplate.

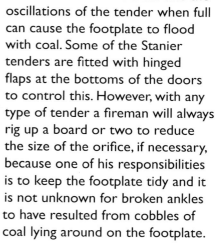

Top: A GWR open-fronted type of tender with the top retaining board in position

Centre: The standard type of GWR tender with the doors closed and some pieces of equipment on the ledge, near the top of the coal space

Bottom: The standard-type GWR tender with the doors open, showing the empty coal space. Note that in GWR tenders the floor of the coal space is at footplate level

Locomotive coals

Next it is necessary to look at the grades of coal suitable for the high rates of steam production required from locomotive boilers. Obviously a high calorific value is essential in order to enable the most compact, and hence the lightest, boiler to be used for a given service requirement, which in itself means that moisture and ash percentages must be low. The quantity of ash produced by combustion is particularly important where long runs between servicings are involved, because steaming becomes impaired as the ash pan approaches full capacity. A low sulphur content is also important, not only because the iron pyrites in which it is present does, in combination with ash of a low fusion temperature, cause the formation of a hard metallic clinker, but also because the inevitable small 'weeps' from a very minor percentage of the thousands of interfaces between the fire and water sides of the boiler, which occur in a cold boiler, result in acid formation and its consequent deleterious effects. Chlorine, which is sometimes present in small quantities, is also to be avoided for the same reason.

One of the biggest problems with early steam locomotives was the production, through incomplete combustion, of large volumes of smoke to the extent that they were required to burn coke instead. However, the *Rocket* boiler of 1829 was the first to incorporate elements to combat this, which proved successful and were retained, with improvements, up to the end of steam locomotive production in this country.

Since smoke is the result of incomplete combustion of the hydrocarbons contained in the volatile matter of the coal, control of it is naturally going to be less of a problem with low volatile coals such as Welsh steam coal. This is why it was used extensively by the Royal Navy in the days of coal-fired warships, because the movement of ships below the horizon could be followed from their smoke trails.

Given the much greater presence of the GWR in South Wales compared with the other major railway companies, and the suitability of Welsh dry steam coals of high calorific value for steam raising in locomotive boilers, it is not surprising that they were the company's main source of fuel. A typical Welsh coal would have of the order of 14% volatile matter, while a high volatile hard coal from the Midlands or Notts/Yorks coalfields might be 36%. The former clearly needs a much higher ratio of primary to secondary air and, because of its slower burning properties, a deeper firebed. To achieve this the air gap between the firebars is wider than on locomotives of the other constituents of the 'Big Four', and the blastpipe arrangements are designed to create a higher smokebox vacuum in order to increase the draught through the firebed. Also, as shown in the firebox diagram, two additional dampers, one in front of and one behind the rear coupled axle, are provided on the 4-6-0 locomotives with that type of grate. No intermediate damper adjustment is normally provided.

It must be assumed that the quality of deep-mined Welsh steam coal was reasonably consistent and always, because of its low volatile matter, required open dampers with no intermediate adjustment necessary in locomotives that have high demands for steam interrupted by periods of little or no demand. By contrast, LMS locomotives, for example, were required to burn more variable qualities of coal and to achieve efficient combustion the dampers were provided with adjustable opening by means of notches (up to five) in the shanks, or levers fitted with pawls operating in notched quadrants (see the accompanying illustration). Dampers return to the closed position unless retained by such means. GWR locomotives such as pannier tanks on which steam demand can vary between high and low dependent on the duties to which it is diagrammed are also fitted with notched damper shanks (see the photograph on the title page).

Quadrant-type damper controls

The final difference in design features between the locomotives under discussion (there are other differences on LNER and SR engines) relate to the firebox door and flap arrangements. Both types of firehole door open by sliding apart on guides and are hollow with air passages to allow the admission of secondary air to the firebox when the doors are closed. Ideally the doors should be closed at all times other than when firing is taking place in order to protect the crew from possible blow-backs or, even worse, some sort of boiler failure.

This is not always possible, particularly with high volatile coals, if anything like efficient combustion is to be achieved. The amount by which the doors are left open depends on the colour of the exhaust at the chimney top, which should be no darker than a light grey. Because the Great Western box is designed for low volatile coal the doors are much thinner than the LMS type because of the requirement for the latter to pass a considerably higher quantity of secondary air.

The GW-type doors each have a semi-circular notch on their inside edge near the top, the purpose of which will be explained later. Both types have a hinged flap that can be raised to partly close the firehole when the doors are open in order to control the ingress of secondary air; the GW type reduces the area by about 70% and the LMS type about 25%.

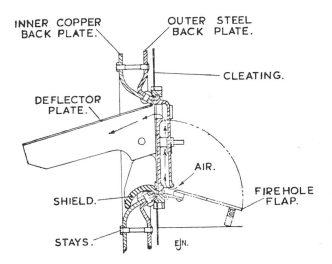

Side view of the GWR firebox door arrangement. E. J. Nutty, courtesy of J. A. Nutty

GWR and LMS firehole door arrangements

GWR: doors open, flap down

LMS: doors open, flap down

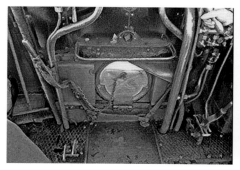

GWR: doors open, flap up

LMS: doors open, flap up

GWR: doors closed, flap down, showing the orifice for the shank of the pricker

LMS: doors closed, flap down

Effects of types of coal on firing methods

It is very useful for a fireman to be able to recognise different types of coal from their appearance and form an opinion of the likely method of firing needed for best results before beginning the journey, although it must be said that coal does not always behave as expected when burning in the firebox.

Good Welsh steam coal is of a bright appearance, is recognisable by its rounded form and is softer than the high volatile coals. However, the lack of bedding planes makes lumps difficult to split with the coal pick and blows from the hammer only result in small fragments being dislodged. It was this characteristic that caused the GWR to retain hand coaling instead of constructing large mechanical coaling plants in which considerable degradation would have resulted from dropping such coal into the bunkers from the heights involved. Because of the low volatile matter content, the coal is slow burning and requires a thick firebed with plenty of primary air.

If the coal is very bright and angular in appearance it is a high volatile (possibly up to 50%), low-ash coal, which ignites and burns very quickly; because a minimum of primary air is required, i.e. a small damper opening, a very thin fire is possible. In some cases with this type of coal sufficient air is admitted to the ashpan through leakage round the damper doors to provide sufficient steam for level working. Thickening of the firebed and some damper opening is only needed to provide the increased steam demand on lengthy gradients and prevent the fire being lifted and discharged through the boiler tubes and flues into the smokebox, with the smaller fragments exiting through the chimney as a result of the heavy exhaust blast.

If the coal is of a similar shape to the above but of a duller appearance, it contains more ash, and in consequence has a lower volatile matter content and burns more slowly, but the ash fusion temperature is normally high and this coal, known as 'Hards', is eminently suitable for steam locomotives. It was mostly mined in the Midlands and Yorkshire coalfields, but Park Hards was available from West Cannock No 5 Colliery at Hednesford up until 1976, and a similar product from Newdigate Colliery, Warwickshire, until about 1980. Until 2013 Daw Mill worked a different area of the same seam, but the quality was more variable and pyrites was sometimes present. The greyer the appearance of this coal, the higher the ash content and the greater the weight, which is apparent by handling it. The ash fusion temperature also tends to be somewhat lower and, if low enough, a soft clinker can form, which sits on the firebars and restricts the primary air if not dealt with, resulting in steaming problems. Hard coals, if delivered in large lumps, can be easily split by the pick and broken by the hammer into a more suitable size for combustion. This is generally recognised to be about that of a man's fist, which is also the ideal size for shovelling. Needless to say, in the days of steam the lazier fireman would not take the trouble to do this if the duty he was on did not require a high rate of steam production.

Because the rate at which any coal burns is determined by the surface area available for oxidation, the smaller the size the greater the surface area for a given weight of coal, and hence quicker combustion. The optimum size is what is known in the trade as Cobbles, the next fraction below being Nuts – a normal size range of 1 inch (25.4mm) up to 2½ inches (63.5mm). Going down to such a size with a high volatile coal on hand-fired steam locomotives, other than shunting engines for example, can result in not being able to control the rate of combustion sufficiently to avoid excessive blowing off. This would be caused by the necessity of using a thicker firebed than that required to meet steam demand, in order to reduce the carry-over of char into the smokebox and prevent consequent steaming problems.

The presence of gold-coloured particles in any coal to be used on a locomotive should put the fireman on his guard, since these are iron pyrites and, unless the ash fusion temperature is high enough, clinker will form. This should be dealt with as soon as possible because it is of a hard metallic nature and the thicker it gets the more difficult it is to remove.

· 9 ·

The fireman's crucial responsibility for safety

Having established the parameters within which the fireman performs his duties, we can consider the change in the importance of his role in steam locomotive operation since the early days. It must be said that the title 'fireman' in no way indicates the extent of the duties now involved and is simply one that has stuck from the days when all that the job entailed was to feed the fire in order to generate steam. In some locomotive designs the fireman even operated from a platform at the opposite end of the locomotive from the driver's footplate.

It was not until engines operating on live steam were being built that any were compact enough to be applied to steam locomotion. By 1829, when *Rocket* was built, boiler pressures had reached 50 pounds per square inch (psi), and to maintain the water level to enable continuous steaming water had to be forced into the boiler against that pressure. This was done by means of water pumps that only operated while the locomotive was in motion, the drive usually being taken from a piston crosshead.

Clearly occasions would arise when a locomotive on a train was halted for some reason or another for a length of time and it became necessary to uncouple it and run it up and down, light engine, in order to restore the boiler water level. Where circumstances prevented light engine movements, it was not unknown for the driving wheel treads to be oiled and, with the tender handbrake hard on, the regulator was opened so that the driving wheels rotated on the spot. It must have been entertaining to watch the driver getting his train away after such an occurrence.

To get back to the subject of the fireman's duties, all this changed in 1859 when a clever French engineer by the name of Gifford invented a device called an injector, which, in its simplest diagrammatic form, is shown in the accompanying illustration.

To operate, the water valve is opened to flood that part of the injector body containing the steam cone. The steam valve is then opened, the high-speed jet of steam is condensed by the surrounding water, and the decrease in the cross-sectional area of the combining cone results in a high-speed jet of hot water entering the delivery cone.

There is a gap between the combining and delivery cones to allow the overflow of excess steam and water during the starting operation. The increase in cross-sectional area of the delivery cone causes the speed of

The live steam injector

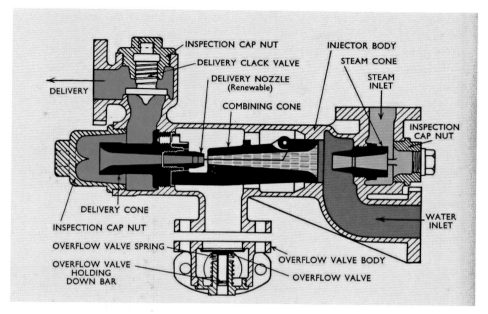

Key

Dark green: feed water   Amber: saturated steam
Light green: water   Green/amber: water and steam

the water jet to rapidly reduce, which converts the kinetic energy on entry into pressure energy at the delivery end, sufficient to overcome the boiler pressure and, via a clack valve, to feed water to the boiler.

The clack valve, which is normally kept shut by the boiler pressure, is opened by the superior pressure developed by the injector and automatically closes when the injector is turned off.

This immediately placed a great deal more responsibility on the fireman than previously because the most important task in the operation of any type of boiler is to maintain the water at a safe level at all times, which, prior to the invention of the injector, was the driver's responsibility. Having said that, the driver is still ultimately responsible for everything that takes place on a locomotive in his charge.

By giving the fireman control of the water feed to the boiler, he could now use this facility to advantage to maintain a more consistent boiler pressure. In fact, the job of the fireman had really become that of boiler manager, but to re-title him seems alien to steam locomotive terminology.

A safe level means keeping the crown plate of the inner firebox covered by an adequate depth of water, and this is made possible by the provision of glass water gauges mounted on the boiler backplate in the cab and positioned so that when the water is just in sight at the bottom of the glass the firebox crown is adequately covered (normally about 3 inches [76mm]). To make sighting of the water level easier, a backing, usually of diagonal black stripes on a white background, is provided, refraction reversing the inclination of the black stripes and indicating the level more clearly.

A fireman taking up a footplate duty, whether the locomotive is already in steam or not, should always satisfy himself that the water gauge(s) is/are indicating correctly by using the shut off/test and drain cocks provided on the gauge frames. Different water levels displayed on locomotives fitted with two gauges should immediately result in further testing.

A fireman preparing his engine on shed before departure should also test both injectors and bring the boiler up to full pressure to check that the safety

A linked GW-type of gauge glass with two test cocks

valves blow off at the registered pressure indicated by the red line on the gauge. Failure to do so must be reported if in excess of 5psi, either above or below.

The gauge glasses are, of course, subject to full boiler pressure and therefore have to be very strong to withstand it. Even so, from time to time they burst without warning, resulting in a loud report that can be quite unnerving, the crew being protected from high-velocity shards of flying glass by the substantial gauge glass protectors. These can consist of metal frames with thick glass sides or metal cages with similar windows. Both types can be detached very quickly from the gauge frame in order to replace the broken glass.

The gauge glass protectors cannot, of course, prevent the discharge of quite large volumes of steam at high pressure into the cab. Suffice to say that the cab fills with steam very rapidly, particularly in cold weather, which can only be stopped by shutting the cocks on the gauge frame. The crew must be able to locate the cocks 'blindfolded' because it is simply impossible to see

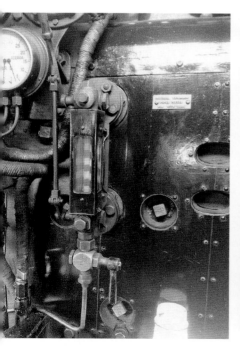

Linked cocks as fitted to BR 'Standard' locomotives

Linked cocks for LMS-type gauge glass protection

them, and protection from scalding to the hands is needed. This can be done, for example, by quickly wrapping a slop jacket (as the overall jacket is usually known) round the fist and shutting off as soon as possible. The normal type of GW fitting makes this task rather safer because the top and bottom cocks are coupled by a link and it is only necessary to drop the handle, which is about 45° from the vertical in the normal position, to 45° below horizontal to achieve this.

On the type mostly used on LMS locomotives, the handles are less accessible and require the one on the top cock to be pulled downwards from vertical to horizontal and that on the bottom cock to be pulled upwards from vertical to horizontal.

LMS locomotives do, however, have the benefit of being fitted with two gauges against the GW, which has only one, but the latter have two additional test cocks in lieu, which can be operated after the main cocks have been closed. I cannot venture an opinion on their effectiveness as, fortunately, I never had a gauge glass fail on a GW locomotive. I have always suspected that the bottom test cock, even when the actual water level in the boiler is above it, would appear to discharge steam when opened because the water would have a tendency to evaporate almost immediately because of its high temperature and the narrow bore of the test cock. While linked cocks make the isolating of the gauge frame easier and safer in the event of a burst sight glass, it can have serious consequences where only one gauge is fitted, as I will explain later, as it also did in at least one case involving two gauges.

However, the advantages of this type of gauge fitting were recognised by BR and applied to the range of 'Standard' locomotives built post-1951, the shortcomings being avoided by fitting two gauges and eliminating the additional test cocks. I conclude that the potential hazard of using linked cocks as demonstrated by a fatal incident in early BR days, of which more later, had either been removed by detailed instructions for running shed fitters and firemen or, preferably, by putting a groove across the square via which each cock is opened and closed to indicate its position.

In British practice the inner firebox is traditionally made of copper, which is a good conductor of heat but also soft and malleable. This latter property makes keeping an adequate depth of water over the firebox crown absolutely essential, so that convection currents can carry heat away from it at a sufficient rate for it to maintain its mechanical integrity.

Since firebox temperatures can be as high as 3,000°F (1,650°C), while the temperature of the water, even in a 250psi boiler, is only 405°F (207°C), the temperature gradient in the firebox plating is very steep.

Ideally the water level should be kept at about three-quarters of a glass and preferably even higher when approaching the summit of a steep climb that is immediately followed by a steep descent. In such cases gravity takes water from the firebox end of the boiler towards the smokebox end and, if the water level is not high enough, can expose the firebox crown plate.

It is of course incumbent upon the fireman to keep a particularly close eye on the boiler water level under such circumstances and maintaining it at the required level, and to

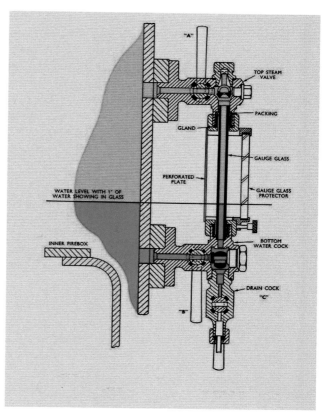

A water gauge with two shut-off/test cocks.

inform the driver of the situation if he is having any trouble due, for example, to steaming problems, the over-enthusiastic use by the driver of the steam available to him, or injector problems. The longer the boiler barrel the more pronounced the effect of any change of gradient becomes, so it is particularly important to maintain a high water level on 'Pacific' locomotives.

The last thing that any locomotive crew wants on a locomotive travelling fast, chimney first downhill, is to have to make an emergency or heavy brake application if the water level is not as high as it might have been, because this also causes the water to surge to the front of the boiler. Slowing down a 400-ton train takes quite a long time and I have no doubt that hearts have been in mouths on the footplate on many occasions until the water has reappeared in the bottom of the glass.

To guard against collapses of the inner firebox, help to cool the fire and alert the crew to take immediate action to drop the fire, brass plugs, normally with a lead core and two or more in number, known as fusible plugs, are screwed into the firebox crown plate. If the crown plate becomes exposed, the cores melt and discharge steam at high pressure into the inner firebox, with the objective of alerting the crew to a serious problem and cooling the fire. Both injectors should be operated in order to keep the boiler water level as high as possible to minimise, or possibly even prevent, damage to the inner firebox, and steps must be taken to drop the fire as quickly as possible.

Failure to maintain the boiler water at a safe level with regard to the current and impending demands for steam and the gradients to be encountered can have very serious consequences. The last boiler barrel explosion in the British Isles occurred on 11 November 1921 and, following the 1923 Grouping that set up the LMS, LNER, GWR and SR, known as the 'Big Four', their Chief Mechanical Engineers established very stringent inspection and maintenance regimes so that no further boiler failure of any kind occurred until 10 November 1940.

The locomotive concerned was streamlined 'Pacific' No 6224 of the 'Princess Coronation' Class (usually referred to as 'Duchesses' these days), hauling the 10.00am Glasgow Central to Euston train loaded to 16 coaches. Evidently the rostered footplate crew had been delayed for some reason and a scratch crew boarded the locomotive only 3 minutes before departure time. Although qualified, neither the driver nor fireman normally worked long-distance express trains and the fireman had never previously fired on a locomotive of this type.

Those who travelled on 'The Coronation Scot' of 12/13 November 2011, run by Vintage Trains and hauled by No 6201 *Princess Elizabeth* to celebrate the 75th Anniversary of its record run (surely the finest feat of steam haulage ever achieved in this country) will be aware that within a few miles of leaving Glasgow, near Uddingston, a steep unremitting climb of some 15 miles commences up to the summit at Craigenhill.

Not surprisingly with this heavy train, the inexperienced fireman was unable to generate steam at the rate at which the engine was using it, with the result that the boiler water level was falling. This is known as 'mortgaging the boiler' and can be used by experienced crews who know exactly what they are doing. Unfortunately, in this case the mortgaging was too severe and although the crew succeeded in getting the train over Craigenhill summit, the sharp change in gradient exposed the firebox crown sheet, resulting in its failure while coasting down the gradient approaching Carstairs. The driver managed to stop the train but both he and the fireman were badly scalded

LMS 'Pacific' No 6201 *Princess Elizabeth. David C. Williams*

by the huge discharge of high-temperature steam. Tragically the poor fireman died later the same day. What the driver should have done, of course, was to have stopped somewhere on the climb, preferably near a signal box, to have a 'blow-up' and recover the water level. However, he was probably concerned about losing further time with such an important train, and therefore decided to continue and hope that nothing would go wrong.

Coincidentally the same locomotive, on the 9.25pm Glasgow-London train of 7 March 1948, also suffered from a firebox crown failure at Lamington, which lies at the bottom of a downhill section some 10 miles further into the journey than the previous incident. On this occasion the cause was both gauges being defective, despite fitters having been called out to them three times in the previous 24 hours.

The locomotive was fitted with two gauges of the linked cocks type, which, because there were two of them, did not require the additional test cocks provided on GWR locomotives. This type also became the normal fitting on BR 'Standard' locomotives, by which time the Achilles heel inherent in the design referred to previously had presumably been removed. In this type the operating arm of the top cock is extended to form a handle that allows the cock to be closed with the hand in a much safer position following a burst gauge glass. A link with forked ends connects the handle to the arm of the lower test cock so that both cocks should open and close simultaneously; both handle and arm fit onto squares at the ends of their cock plugs.

Since the angle between open and closed is 90°, therein was the Achilles heel. After dismantling for repair or re-packing (this used to be done with loose asbestos), it was possible to reassemble with one cock open while the other was closed. This had happened on this occasion and the water gauge so coupled had been thought to be the one giving the correct reading.

The locomotive crew in this case were completely blameless and totally unaware of the impending disaster, which occurred when the firebox crown sheet gave way. It did not split but had become softened to the extent that it was forced over 21 riveted stay heads and pulled the stay nuts off three others (see the illustration below).

Even though the inner firebox had not collapsed, the discharge of steam through the 24 stay holes exposed was sufficient to inflict terrible scalds and burns on the footplate crew, and in this case the driver's injuries proved to be fatal.

These two incidents alone show how critical boiler management and maintenance are to the safe operation of steam locomotives.

I have previously referred to the use of fusible plugs in the firebox crown plate, so readers may have wondered why they do not appear to have had any effect in preventing these two fatal accidents. In the first one it has to be

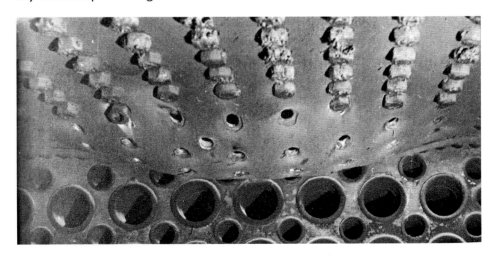

A collapsed firebox crown. *British Railways*

assumed that the crew, bearing in mind that there was no report of the water gauges being faulty, were aware that the water level was too low but hoped that they could get away with it; also that at least one of the fusible plugs had melted on the descent from the summit, but they knew that only half a mile beyond Carstairs was three-quarters of a mile of level track followed by 2¼ miles rising at 1 in 150 on which they could have brought the train to a halt with the boiler water lying towards the firebox end and possibly averted a disaster.

In the second case the crew had already heard the sound of escaping steam by Uddingston, some 9 miles from Glasgow, and at Carstairs a foreman and two fitters were summoned from the running shed. Because the right-hand gauge glass was showing almost full and the locomotive had travelled 20 miles since the noise was first heard, they had no reason to suspect that a fusible plug had blown. Because of the configuration of the firebox, it would have been the front one furthest from the firehole door, and in such a large firebox it might have been difficult to spot anyway, so unfortunately the locomotive was allowed to carry on, with tragic consequences.

· 10 ·
The basics of firing

No other machine in history has ever been designed in which the performance and efficiency is so dependent upon the persons operating it as the steam locomotive, nor now ever will be. Of the crew, the fireman can have the greatest influence on these characteristics and that is why The Craft of the Fireman is so important.

This is complicated by the fact that a peculiarity of steam locomotives that no one has ever been able to satisfactorily explain is why, out of a batch of engines of the same type, built by the same makers to the same specification at the same time, some will be very different from the rest, either freer running, stronger on the banks, better steaming, or other characteristics. Put these variations together with numerous locomotive designs that have different fireboxes, grates, ash pans, damper arrangements (for example some LMS engines up to Class 3 have only one damper), weight of train relative to locomotive size and power, grades of coal, weather conditions and so on, and it is clear that there are so many variables requiring different methods of firing to get the best results that it is not possible to teach anyone how to fire a locomotive. It all comes down to experience and the mental approach of the fireman. I am sorry to say that some firemen never learn, although they manage to get by, but that is not what The Craft of the Fireman is all about.

There are some basics, however, that a fireman needs to know. For example, air behaves in exactly the same way as electricity, i.e. the lower the resistance the greater the flow, so if there are any weak spots in the firebed, the airflow will be greater in those areas. If not dealt with this can cause holes to develop, affecting steaming due to the cold air entering the firebox. Perhaps even more importantly, cold draughts on very hot firebox tube plates inevitably cause additional work for the boilersmiths.

Such problems should be avoided if the fire is carefully built up before starting away. If the blower is turned up, hot spots will develop where the air is passing through the firebed more easily and coal should be added at these points. At this stage the fire is quite cool and the surface of the firebed can be observed. A uniform colour throughout means that the fire can be built up to the thickness required for the duty concerned.

This thickness should always be at a minimum if highest efficiency is to be achieved, so there is always a slight risk of a hole developing at some stage when working the train. If the engine is working hard with a relatively thin fire, the fire should be a dazzling white and the presence of a hole may only become apparent by a loss in steam pressure. If under easy steam the fire is cooler with a yellow appearance, and a thin spot is indicated by a red area; if a hole is forming, it appears first at the top of the firebed, and the coal surfaces on the inside of the hole can be seen glowing a dull red from the cooling effect, and should receive immediate attention. It is possible to examine the state of the fire over the flat part of the grate even when reasonably hot, if so desired, by using the firing shovel inverted in the firehole to direct a stream of cold air on to the surface of the fire.

A 'must' is to have what is called a 'back' on the fire. It is usual to have a damper door in the ashpan below the firehole. This enables a thicker firebed to be used across the back of the grate and the top layer of the sloping firebed tends to migrate forwards due to the oscillations of the locomotive, thus helping the fireman, as does the cooler temperature in the vicinity of the firehole.

With this basic knowledge, the fireman, if he applies himself properly to the task, can become proficient at it. Of course things are now vastly different from steam days when cleaners became passed cleaners and commenced firing in the shunting links. Nowadays prospective firemen often act as support crew and get some footplate practice in until considered sufficiently proficient to be passed out to fire on main-line charters. Others come qualified as firemen on preserved railways but still have to pass out.

For his first few turns (each rostered footplate duty is known as a turn) he will probably only have one concern on his mind – that of not 'going down the nick', i.e. running short of steam and having to stop for a blow-up. Once he has got some confidence, if he intends to become a craftsman at the art he must address other issues, which I will detail later.

All the preserved railways, of necessity, started operating with a nucleus of professional footplatemen, but usually too few to provide cover other than in the short term. Naturally a number of volunteers had aspirations to become firemen and, perhaps, eventually drivers. To this end, railways organised courses for prospective firemen from senior members of the cleaning and disposal links. On the Severn Valley Railway, where I was a volunteer, these were held on Sunday mornings, but due to the amount of weekend work involved with my job, I was unable to attend.

However, since the SVR planned to extend operations to Bewdley in 1974, additional firemen were going to be needed, so I informed the Operating Superintendent and Shedmaster, a Crewe-trained man by the name of Arthur Francis Stewart Becker (now deceased), that I had done some firing (unofficial) on industrial locomotives on very severe gradients. As a result he gave me a Rule Book and said that if I could pass the SVR footplate inspector (the late Jack Beaman) on the rules for firemen, he would give me a practical footplate test.

Having been successful on the Rules, my footplate practical test was arranged for New Year's Day 1974. As I was attending solely for that purpose, I did not assist with the preparation and only presented myself when the locomotive, No 193 (an 'Austerity' 0-6-0ST) was on the train, which consisted of only four coaches. As I was capable of firing an 'Austerity' competently with a load 50% greater on gradients twice as steep as Eardington Bank, I felt confident that I should not have any problems.

The locomotive crew were David Johnson (driver) and Graham Nangreave (fireman), both unfortunately now deceased. I got on the footplate and had a quick look at the water and pressure gauges and the condition of the fire. I knew that the coal was high volatile and, being fairly small cobbles, could be flashed up quickly, so there was plenty of time.

We therefore started to chat and I soon noticed David glancing at the pressure gauge from time to time. Before long he asked, 'Aren't you going to put any coal on?'

Now the ideal situation for leaving a station on a rising gradient with a cold engine is to have a hot fire resulting from building the fire at the correct rate with the pressure just coming up to the red line at departure time. I had judged it pretty well and we had plenty of steam on the 1-mile climb, mostly at 1 in 100, off the platform end up to Eardington summit. Apart from the acceleration from the 5mph slack at Sterns, there is no great demand for steam as far as Hampton Loade. I made the fire up for the 1 in 145 climb out of the station, which took us to Sterns, and the length of the slack gave adequate time to make up the fire for Eardington Bank. I am pleased to say that the needle remained on the red line all the way, with no blowing off, and the bottom of the firehole doors a dull red. After arrival at Bridgnorth, Graham was kind enough to say, 'You're a better fireman than I am!'

The test had turned out to be a total success, so Arthur made arrangements for me to be examined by Arthur Bullock, the BR footplate inspector, on 21 April. The locomotive concerned was No 5764, the pannier tank, and I am pleased to say that I was again successful. As there were footplate vacancies at that time, there was no grade of Passed Cleaner, so I immediately became a fireman and had my first turn on No 43106 in May 1974.

In my particular circumstances I now consider it to have been an advantage not to have been on the footplate course since I had already studied Fuel Technology and been involved in the mining industry for 22 years. I therefore already had a good knowledge of coal and its efficient combustion, and was therefore able to apply this knowledge to firing with a completely open mind.

GWR 0-6-0 pannier tank No 5764. *David C. Williams*

Improving technique

I deliberately titled this book *The Craft of the Fireman* because top-class firing is a craft, and to craft anything is, by definition, 'to produce by painstaking skill and attention to detail'. The product of the fireman is his firing performance and if he is totally satisfied just because he has provided sufficient steam to allow the driver to make an exhilarating run, he will never become a top-class fireman.

To do that requires the steam to be produced under the following constraints:
• Never make black smoke
• Never blow off other than testing the safety valves against the registered pressure on the gauge (indicated by a red line) before leaving the shed
• Keep the boiler pressure within 10psi of blowing off at all times when steam is required

The importance of not wasting, in the form of black smoke, the valuable hydrocarbons that have four times the calorific value of the fixed carbon on the grate has already been stressed.

Blowing off wastes both coal and water, and for a locomotive of the size of a 'Hall' or a 'Black Five' this amounts to at least 10lb (4.54kg) of coal and 8 gallons (36.4l) of water per minute. Safety valves are designed to shut off virtually instantaneously as the pressure drops below the registered figure, but occasionally, perhaps due to excessive friction in the valve spindle, they stick open. In some cases this can cause a reduction of 10psi or more before shutting off, which can take a considerable time dependent on the rates at which the boiler is steaming and the driver is using that steam. In these circumstances, to avoid excessive waste the fireman must make doubly sure that he never allows the boiler to blow off. Although not dangerous, failure to shut off more than 5psi below the registered pressure must also be reported.

The higher the pressure in the boiler, the shorter the cut-off (the point at which steam supply to the cylinders is stopped by the valves) that can be employed by the driver using the expansive property of the steam to propel the pistons until the exhaust ports open, thus increasing efficiency.

The three objectives mentioned above must be targeted on each firing turn in order to improve personal performance, and the fireman must become his own severest critic if he is to reach the top. To meet all three objectives, the fireman has, effectively, to perform a balancing act that becomes more difficult on duties in which intermittent demands for steam are required.

A fireman must have his fire in the right condition to supply steam when required, and the boiler water and fire at such levels that he can put the injector(s) on to avoid blowing off when it is not. Although the feed water is hot after passage through the injector(s), it is still considerably cooler than the water in the boiler, so the use of the injector(s) reduces the rate of steam production and will prevent blowing off, provided the fireman has left sufficient room in the boiler and controlled the rate of combustion in the firebox.

A degree of anticipation is needed because the fire is usually at its hottest at the time steam demand is reduced to a minimum as the regulator is closed. With a grate area of 27.1sq ft (2.52sq m) on a 'Hall' and 29.45sq ft (2.73sq m) on a 'Castle', the fires take some time to cool down. Some firemen tend to overfill the boiler to avoid excessive blowing off if they have misjudged and are carrying too large a fire. This can lead to priming after the driver has again put on steam, particularly so if a gradient requiring a wide regulator opening is to be climbed and the boiler is due for a washout. Priming happens when water is carried over to the cylinders with the steam, and unless the driver shuts off steam quickly and opens the drain cocks damage to the motion can result.

Water is incompressible, as was vividly demonstrated at Hereford one morning in October 1980 when we, as back-up crew (now known as support crew), were preparing LMS Stanier 'Black Five' No 5000 to work the 'Red Dragon', double-heading with LMS Ivatt 'Mogul' No 43106. The time came to move No 5000 and it eased forward about a yard (0.91m) when the driving wheels locked solid and the locomotive skidded forward a few inches before stopping. The cause was a blocked front drain cock on the fireman's side.

LMS 'Black Five'
4-6-0 No 5000.
David C. Williams

As I have already indicated, some firemen do not practice the art of firing, but for those who do it really is a craft, as defined. Unfortunately, to demonstrate that this is so requires detailed explanation, which is going to take time and space. In a nutshell, the craft is to manage a boiler within tight limits in order to achieve maximum output when required with high efficiency, no matter what the circumstances.

The best environment in which to gain a wide experience quickly is on a preserved railway of reasonable length, e.g. 12 miles or more, with some testing gradients, a number of booked stops and speed restrictions creating an intermittent demand for steam, a variety of locomotive types and coals, and realistic loads, say eight coaches.

The Severn Valley Railway satisfied all those requirements during the years I was on the footplate. Apart from a short period before May 1974, the route mileage was 12½ to Bewdley and, from 1983, 16¼ to Kidderminster. As regards gradients, Eardington Bank, from a 5mph slack at Sterns (now 15mph), is 1¾ miles at 1 in 100 apart from a short easing through Eardington station platform. The climb to Foley Park starts at Bewdley South Junction for 1½ miles, the last mile of which is at 1 in 100, and the northbound starts from Arley, Highley and Hampton Loade are all on rising gradients. The first 1¼ miles out of Bridgnorth are mostly rising at 1 in 100.

With regard to locomotives, we were spoiled. The smaller ones started to arrive in March 1967, but LMS 8F No 48773 and 'Black Five' No 45110, both in operating condition, came in January 1969 and August 1970 respectively. The big War Department 2-10-0 No 600 *Gordon* emerged after overhaul in Bridgnorth Works in 1971, if my memory serves me correctly. Eventually I fired and drove 22 different classes of locomotive, from the GWR, LMS, LNER, SR, BR and the WD.

We also had a number of different qualities of coal from sources such as Granville Colliery in Shropshire, West Cannock No 5 Colliery in Cannock Chase, Snibston Colliery in Leicestershire, Newdigate Colliery in Warwickshire, and several collieries in South Wales including Oakdale, and even some opencast from Bryn Pica.

I believe all these factors provided the ideal circumstances in which to improve the art of firing.

The dimensions of a locomotive that have the greatest effect on steam

LMS 8F 2-8-0 No 48773. *David C. Williams*

demand are cylinder volume and wheel diameter, and these, coupled with boiler dimensions, largely govern the method of firing required.

A comparison between locomotives of a similar size using the same type of high volatile coal will illustrate this. Take the GW pannier tank No 5764, the LMS small Ivatt 2-6-0 No 46443 and the WD 'Austerity' 0-6-0ST No 193. Of these, the pannier has the smallest grate at 15.3sq ft, but a deep firebox, 17½in by 24in cylinders, and a 4 ft 7½in driving wheel diameter. For the 2-6-0 the corresponding figures are 17.5sq ft, 16in by 24in and 5ft 0in, and for the 'Austerity' 16.75sq ft, 18in by 26in and 4 ft 3in.

The heat is transferred to the boiler water through the walls and crown plate of the inner firebox, known as the firebox heating surface, and the boiler tubes/flues in the boiler barrel. In the case of the pannier the heating surfaces are 102sq ft and 1,075sq ft respectively, totalling 1,177sq ft; for the 2-6-0 they are 101sq ft and 924sq ft respectively, totalling 1,025sq ft; and for the WD 87sq ft and 873sq ft respectively, totalling 960sq ft.

So, assuming the thermal efficiency to be the same, for a given weight of train, gradient, speed and type of coal, the pannier, although helped by its greater total evaporative surface, will need to burn more coal per square foot of grate area than the 2-6-0 with its smaller cylinders, larger-diameter driving wheels and bigger grate. (The latter also has a superheated boiler, but I do not intend to go into the benefits of superheating in a book about firing.) The odd man out is the 'Austerity', with the biggest cylinders, the smallest driving wheels and the lowest evaporative surface area. As the design specification was for a powerful shunting engine capable of moving 1,000-ton trains, it was obviously not the ideal type for passenger work.

Of the former two, the pannier with its small grate and deep firebox is the easier to fire. The grate is flat and once the fire is made up, thicker across the back of the grate above the damper, not much more than dropping shovelsful of coal into the corners is required, forming what is known as a saucer-shaped fire which, as its name implies, has a concave surface. Of course the fire must

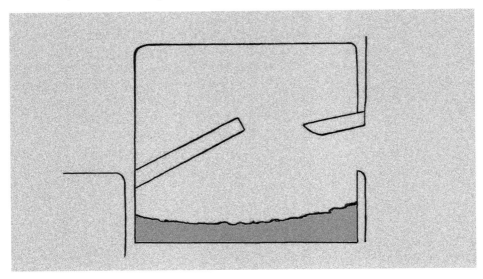

A GW pannier tank firebed

not be allowed to get too thin in the middle of the grate, otherwise a hole can develop if the engine is working hard.

The 'Mogul' has a slightly sloping grate and all that it requires is a fire thicker under the door and tapering down towards the front throughout, but requires more accuracy with the shovel. The boiler is free steaming and I remember on one occasion being able, with a high volatile coal, to fire the engine with the damper closed, there being sufficient leakage through the ashpan to provide all the primary air required other than when more steam was needed for the banks and starting from station stops on adverse gradients.

Ivatt 2-6-0 No 46443.
David C. Williams

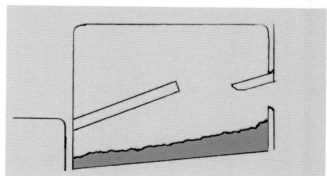

The Ivatt 'Mogul'
firebed

You will not be surprised to know, looking at the boiler dimensions compared with those of the cylinders and driving wheels, that shortage of steam could be a problem with the 'Austerity'. Under such circumstances drivers tended to ease the regulator, which, given the above dimensions, is counterproductive and can only lead to 'going down the nick', i.e. stopping for a 'blow-up'. The combination of a small grate area, large cylinders and small wheels means that more steam has to be produced per square foot of grate area, which can only be achieved by burning more coal per square foot, so a thicker firebed is required. This makes it more resistant to the flow of primary air required for combustion. How can it be overcome? By working the engine hard enough to increase the smokebox vacuum sufficiently to do so. So the

Above: 'Austerity'
0-6-0ST No 193
Shropshire.
David C. Williams

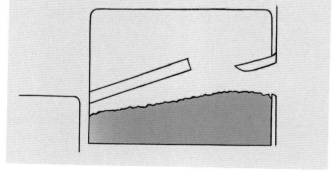

Right: The 'Austerity'
0-6-0ST firebox

recipe was: build a good deep fire and thrash the engine, which was also of course a recipe for great entertainment. The deep hot fire that resulted then provided sufficient steam where only small regulator openings were required. 'Austerities' are well known for having a stentorian bark, and to hear No 193 storming Eardington bank on full regulator was a sound never to be forgotten.

It just so happens that circumstances arose in 1977 that enabled a spectacularly noisy run to be made with this locomotive, now named *Shropshire.* Driver Dave Cooke was emigrating to New Zealand and I was rostered as fireman on his last turn, which was off Bridgnorth. Quite naturally he was looking to finish on a highlight, so I told him I would try and provide all the steam he could use. As the date was early autumn, we had an off-peak loading of six coaches only.

The first inkling of events being in our favour was when the guard came up to the footplate at Bewdley and asked us to stop at the Victoria Bridge in order for the now dismantled frontier post building from the filming of *The Seven Per Cent Solution* to be loaded into the brake.

We knew that this would take some time, so Dave set off with considerable vigour but, approaching Northwood Halt, we saw a would-be passenger indicating that he wished to board the train. Northwood has always been a request stop, but it was quite unusual to have a northbound passenger.

This additional short delay, coupled with the much longer one at the Victoria Bridge, meant that we were well behind schedule at Arley, so fast running was required to get us to Hampton Loade on time to cross the other service train. From Hampton Loade timetable considerations no longer apply as an early arrival in Bridgnorth is of no consequence. As the locomotive was steaming well, Dave was really able to enjoy himself and, due to its small wheels and the speed at which we were travelling, we simply roared up Eardington Bank.

Soon after we arrived at Bridgnorth, a passenger rushed up to the locomotive to congratulate us on a fantastic run. He wore a brushed-back hairstyle that was well encrusted with char, so I replied, 'I can see that you enjoyed it.'

Our overall time, start to stop, was 50 minutes, but the two additional stops cost at least 9 minutes, giving a net time of 41 minutes against the current timetable allowance of 53 minutes.

This was undoubtedly the fastest run between Bewdley and Bridgnorth ever achieved by *Shropshire* during its time on the Severn Valley Railway, proving it to be more than capable of handling any of the services, provided it was fired and driven correctly.

However, its small driving wheels, together with large cylinders and limited water capacity, meant that it was not really suitable motive power for the SVR and was allowed to leave.

I trust that these three examples of the differences in firing needed on locomotives of very similar size, using the same type of coal and performing the same duty, have given some idea of why a fireman must adapt his methods to suit the circumstances. When you remember that to become a real craftsman this also has to be done within the constraints of the three objectives listed above, the degree of difficulty is readily apparent.

The final example that I am about to give illustrates the gulf between the two extremes. It occurred one Saturday afternoon in late summer 1974 when the fireman booked for the relief turn had failed to show up and I was given the opportunity of replacing him. The locomotive involved was War Department 2-10-0 No 600 *Gordon*, the footplate of which I had never previously been on with the loco in steam.

War Department 2-10-0 No 600 *Gordon. David C. Williams*

Gordon is massive compared with the three locomotives already discussed, with a wide firebox having a grate area of 40sq ft (3.72sq m) i.e. nearly 2½ times bigger than the largest of the others, a 225psi boiler to match, and 19in by 28in cylinders. I had a quick look round, bearing in mind that the call did not come until shortly before departure time, and was surprised, to say the least, that there were no damper controls on the footplate. I found them, unusually, on the sides of the ashpan, two on each side with adjustable doors that could be locked in the desired position. As these were all open, I decided to leave them as they were and see how the grate performed out on the road.

Due to its size and power, I knew that the locomotive would not have to be worked very hard and, with that large grate, primary air velocity through the firebed would be low so a very thin fire could be used. With no damper control available to me, this would be very desirable if I was to manage the boiler without blowing off. Nevertheless, the same rules of keeping the back corners filled and not allowing holes to develop still applied. The grates on these wide-firebox locomotives are all around 7 feet (2.13m) in width, more than twice the width of the grate in a narrow box. In later years two 'Pacifics', which also have wide fireboxes, SR 'West Country' No 34027 *Taw Valley* and LNER 'A4' No 60009 *Union of South Africa*, also made their homes on the SVR (the latter later left to concentrate on main-line running). The trick would be to feed the back corners, and I found that by rotating the shaft of the shovel while the blade was passing through the firehole and finishing with a sideways flick as the full blade entered the firebox, the coal could be heard hitting the side of the box before dropping into the corner. I used a shallow saucer-shaped fire, thicker along the side waterwalls, because of the damper locations, and this proved to be satisfactory.

It has to be said that, from time to time, things do not always go according to plan and, for no apparent reason, the engine does not steam properly. On these occasions it is up to the fireman to engage his brain and by observation of the condition of the fire, the exhaust and the setting of the boiler controls, try to work out how to improve matters.

13

Honing skills

I will now mention an incident that, from an efficiency point of view, was insignificant, but to a fireman intent on perfecting the art was important. On the approach to Bewdley station I noted that the pressure gauge needle was creeping up towards the red line, and I was going to put on the injector when I saw the North Box signalman standing on the foot crossing waiting for the single-line token to be delivered to him instead of me dropping it onto the token-catcher on the opposite side of the train. It is bad practice to be using an injector while passing close to someone on the ground, particularly under braking when some injectors have a tendency to blow out and discharge a jet of scalding steam and water, so I delayed setting it until I had surrendered the token. Although I got it on immediately, it was a fraction too late and the driver's side safety valve lifted just as we passed under the footbridge.

This may seem of no consequence to the average observer, but a top-class fireman always has his boiler under control so that it does not blow off at any point where he knows the train is going to stop. Any fireman aiming to reach the top therefore has to guard against such minor blemishes, and I should have anticipated that the signalman might be on the crossing and set the injector well in advance so that I could have shut it off prior to surrendering the token. However, I was pleased when, having disposed, the driver, Dave Lacey, congratulated me on my performance. I was pleasantly surprised to find that lack of damper adjustment did not prove to be a problem since, with a thin fire, minor adjustments to the firebed depth, together with use of the injector, provided sufficient control.

Continually practising firing within the already mentioned three constraints meant that my boiler control steadily improved, and by the beginning of 1978 I set myself the target of 12 months of firing turns without blowing off. Everything went according to plan until the third Saturday in September, the Saturday of the Enthusiasts' Weekend as it used to be called in the days before preserved railways began to have Galas.

I was firing to the late John Hurley, an old Oxley driver, on LMS 8F No 8233 working off Bridgnorth, and as we came to the top of the short climb up through Eymore Wood cutting from the Victoria Bridge, I set the injector in anticipation of him easing the regulator past Trimpley Reservoir. I sat down just enjoying the ride when suddenly the safety valve lifted with no prior warning such as a heavy 'feather'. I put the second injector on, which stopped the blowing off almost immediately, so the wastage of coal and water was minimal, but this was not important. What was important was that, after almost nine months of success, I had failed to meet one of my objectives for 1978 through a moment's inattention. Because I had never previously needed a second injector at this point, I wrongly assumed that I had the boiler under perfect control and did not bother to consult the pressure gauge with the above disappointing consequence. It also taught me the lesson that just because something has never happened previously when operating a steam locomotive, that does not mean it will not happen in the future. Constant vigilance is required so that any changes can be noted and acted upon.

With regard to the other two objectives, I have to admit that smoke was sometimes darker than it should be and I did not always manage to keep pressure within the 10psi range that I had set as a target, although I did not miss it by any significant amount. Unless running under stable conditions, when it is possible for an injector to be set to maintain the boiler water at a consistent level, it is necessary in order to manage the boiler within a range of 10psi to make frequent use of it for short periods. Some drivers do not like this because they consider that it wastes water during the short period of time between the water valve being opened and the steam picking the water up. In fact, when using tenders with a quick-action stopcock such as the Stanier type, which only take about a second to open, and with the injector feed valve set to the optimum position, pick-up is almost instantaneous when the injector steam valve is opened. Of course I carried on with the same objectives in 1979, but never achieved them because I was promoted to driver in June of that year, vacancies meaning that there was no grade of passed fireman at that time.

Writing this section has reminded me of a long-forgotten incident that illustrates the single-mindedness required in a fireman in attempting to perfect, if that is at all possible, the art of firing. A musician aiming for the top can, almost without exception, practise on the chosen instrument as much as he/she desires. A locomotive fireman can only practise when the opportunity of footplate work arises.

The incident some time in 1978/79 concerned GWR 'Hall' Class No 6960 *Raveningham Hall* being returned light engine from Bewdley to Bridgnorth. We must have been on an unbalanced working, which then involved a Bewdley shunting operation that meant we were too late to couple up to the Bridgnorth-bound service train. However, because this had booked stops at Arley and Highley, we arrived at the latter station while the service train was still in the section to Hampton Loade.

We happened to be giving a lift back to Bob Florence, the custodian of Andrew Barclay 0-4-0ST *Invicta*, ex-Chatham Dockyard. As usual the passenger was allowed to sit on the fireman's seat and the obligatory footplate chat was going on while we were waiting for the token when Bob turned towards me and the following exchange took place. With tongue in cheek he asked, 'Does that pressure gauge work?'

'Yes, why?'

'Well, the needle has never moved off the red line yet.'

Now everybody must know that to work light engine, boiler pressure does not need to be anywhere near the red line, but to practise boiler management even on a light engine working I decided not to give myself the latitude of 10psi below full pressure, as I did with passenger trains, but attempted to keep it on the mark at all times without ever blowing off. After all, steam demand required to move 120 tons is considerably less than that for around 400 tons, but every footplate turn must be regarded as a challenge if a fireman is really intent on honing his firing skills to the ultimate. Fortunately, as tested during preparation, the safety valves were blowing off a pound or two heavy, so that even with the needle on the mark they were only lightly feathering.

Of course, for this duty only a very thin fire was needed, basically just keeping the grate covered and burning it off on Eardington Bank to provide a very easy disposal at Bridgnorth.

I apologise for going on at such length, but unfortunately it is necessary to do so in order to demonstrate the difference between perfectly adequate firing and the craft of top-class firemanship, which, as I hope I have already shown, is much easier to write about than to achieve.

Given the variety of both locomotives and coal, coupled with the faster timings in the 1970s, the SVR was an ideal location for a fireman wishing to improve his boiler management skills. Any serious delay to one train with four or five trains in the circuit, and intermediate passing places only at Hampton Loade and Arley, meant speeding, where it was safe to do so, was necessary in order to get back on time.

A much more relaxed attitude towards it existed at that time and this gave drivers an excuse to work locomotives really hard. For example, on one occasion in 1978 I was firing on GWR No 6960 *Raveningham Hall* to a BR driver who shall be nameless, and he worked the train up to 45mph on the 'racing stretch' between Northwood and Bewdley. Admittedly this was aided by a fairly liberal interpretation of the 10mph restriction at Northwood Crossing but, as it predated the installation of the flashing lights, a flagman was on duty and it was safe to do so. Another driver claimed 48mph with BR

BR 'Standard' 2-6-4T No 80079. *David C. Williams*

'Standard' Class 4 2-6-4T No 80079, all of this happening with a Light Railway Order speed limit of 25mph. It was, however, excellent training for firemen.

It must be stressed that these very high speeds were extremely rare and were obtained by some drivers using the excuse of regaining time in order to determine the maximum speed that could be reached in a particular section.

However, 35 to 40mph became quite common and in the late 1970s the amount of speeding occurring became a concern for the SVR Guarantee Company, the operating body, so duly appeared on the Agenda at one of the Board Meetings. At the time I was a director of SVR (Holdings) plc and there was in being a reciprocal arrangement for members of each Board to attend the other Board's meetings, allowing full discussion but not voting rights. It was decided to make an informal approach to the late Major P. M. Olver, HM Inspecting Officer for railways, concerning the possibility of raising the limit to 40mph. Now Major Olver was an experienced practical railwayman, and his response was, 'You are doing 40 now. If I give you 40 you will be doing 60!' Effectively he was saying that he was prepared to turn a blind eye to it, being confident that the drivers were responsible enough to only speed where it was safe to do so. This allayed the concerns of the Guarantee Board for the time being, and things continued much as before.

In the heyday of main line steam, there were many well-known drivers.

What is surprising is that so few firemen were known by name, given that none of the great performances could have been achieved without firing of the highest class, so it is a pity that most did not receive the accolade that they deserved. Fortunately, the importance of the fireman's performance is given much greater recognition these days.

Things are different now of course, compared with how they were in the days of steam. For many footplatemen it was just a way of earning a living and it is only human nature to make the job as easy as possible. At the other end of the scale you had some footplate staff who took such a pride in their performance that in order to reach even higher standards they voluntarily attended Mutual Improvement Classes (known as MICs and organised by the footplatemen themselves to further footplate knowledge) on Sunday mornings, without pay, at their locomotive running sheds, even when a six-day working week was the norm.

Today we have footplate crews who do it because of their love of steam locomotives, not just to earn their bread and butter, so they are interested in footplate work. This, coupled with the locomotives being kept in top-class condition, owners or owning groups liking to experience their machines being extended, passengers travelling for enjoyment and not out of necessity, and numerous train-timers providing even more of an incentive for footplate crews, has resulted in a golden age of steam running such that none of us could have ever anticipated after 11 August 1968, or even after the return to steam in October 1971. On several occasions the best-known performances of locomotives of certain classes in the days of steam have been exceeded. Make the most of it while you still can.

Readers may well be amazed, however, when I suggest that the firing turns on the magnificent and in some ways almost unbelievable running of 'The Bristolian' in April 2010 were probably among the easiest that Vintage Trains' firemen have ever experienced, particularly on the return leg from Bristol to Paddington. This was because steam demand on the boiler must not only have been very consistent, but also relatively low for about 100 miles.

Although speed was in the 70-plus range throughout, on 'Brunel's billiard table' with a light load, my guess is that only first valve of the regulator with cut-off of 15-20% would be required. Under these conditions a good exhaust injector can normally be trimmed to feed the boiler at the rate required to maintain the water level, thus obviating the necessity for regular starting and stopping of injectors and, despite the speed, the rate of firing needed would not have been particularly high. I should imagine that the fireman spent rather more of the journey time enjoying the ride than is possible on most normal firing turns, as the coal consumption per mile should have been lower than anything previously achieved.

In addition, the boiler conditions would be at their most stable, such that a rhythm of firing emerges, and the level of vigilance normally required with continually changing conditions can be relaxed.

As there is absolutely no substitute for main-line running, nor ever could be, it is not surprising that some experienced firemen from the longer preserved lines are now itching for such work and a number, having passed the requisite tests, are taking main-line turns.

Good boiler management is the same wherever it is practised, so that an experienced fireman from one of the longer preserved railways, where the turn can consist of locomotive preparation, 80 miles or so of firing, followed by disposal, should have no difficulty in taking a main-line turn. The only difference is that the rate of firing required on the main line is, of course, considerably higher, but boiler management is easier because the demand for steam is normally less intermittent. Exceptions are very tricky routes such as the Central Wales line, which has a saw-tooth gradient profile and various stops for one reason or another, which makes achieving the three objectives of top-class firing extremely difficult.

Firemen regularly working over the same route as on the longer preserved railways naturally know the gradient profile in intimate detail, and this is essential if a good firing performance is to be achieved. Any fireman working a main-line turn must make sure that he either knows the gradient profile or has a diagram of it available. It is also important to obtain the working schedule showing booked operational and watering stops so that, demand for steam or not, as the case may be, can be anticipated because of the time taken to reduce from high to almost negligible rates of steam production and vice versa. In other words, fires must be built up in advance of high steam demands and running-down of the fire must commence at some point during those demands to avoid blowing off after the regulator is closed or eased.

The serious photographer is always in pursuit of that elusive master-shot, and the serious fireman likewise the perfect firing turn. In doing so he is aware that he is actually making the job more demanding for himself. As we have seen with 'The Bristolian', stable conditions make life easier for the fireman (other than long steep gradients of course), but unfortunately the circumstances that provide those stable conditions rarely exist.

Every time the firehole doors are opened, when the secondary air is already adequate for complete combustion, the cooling effect reduces the steaming rate slightly, which is further reduced by adding a round of coal to the firebed. With a high volatile coal and a hot fire, the discharge and burning of as much of the hydrocarbons as possible before they are wasted by exiting through the chimney can compensate for this provided that coal is only added in small quantities. The fireman not bothered about efficiency will put on a heavier round of coal, followed by shutting the firebox doors to keep the footplate as cool as possible, and ignoring the black or dark smoke. It will of course clear itself when the bulk of the hydrocarbons has been driven off the firebed, but a much higher percentage of their calorific value will have been wasted. When using the injector he will allow himself more latitude with steam pressure, allowing it to drop to perhaps 30psi or more below maximum. The resultant loss in the efficiency of working the locomotive means he will have to shovel more coal into the firebox, but many firemen are willing to trade this for longer periods spent sitting on the seat and enjoying the ride.

On the other hand, the fireman in search of perfection will use the 'little and often' firing technique, thereby reducing the cooling effect and also the amount of hydrocarbons produced at each firing. He will regularly observe the exhaust at the chimney top and make small reductions in the gap between the firehole doors in order to provide, as nearly as possible, the correct amount of secondary air for complete combustion. Of course, the doors can be fully closed much more quickly than when heavy rounds are employed. The injector will be used more frequently in order to keep within 10psi of the red line without blowing off. Wherever the opportunity arises, he will attempt to trim the injector to the steaming rate, but some injectors have a limited range of adjustment and others only appear to work properly at one rate of feed. Needless to say, he will use the exhaust injector, if fitted, which only uses waste steam as against the live steam injector, in locations where the regulator is likely to be open for a reasonable time.

To keep on top of all this means that the fireman is very busy with little time to relax. Pursuit of the perfect firing turn is like a New Year Resolution, never to be broken. I use the term advisedly because if a fireman taking a firing turn decides for once to abandon the personal rigid discipline needed for continuous vigilance followed by appropriate action, he may well find that he enjoys himself more than usual. As a consequence he may decide that he is happy with his firing ability and the Resolution, as usual, is not resurrected. That does not mean that his ability will not improve further because, like in many other spheres, experience is all-important, and a good fireman who can solve the problems that arise from time to time will always become more competent. He will not, however, reach the pinnacle of the art.

14

Differences between firing low and high volatile coals

The time is long overdue for considering the actual burning of coal in locomotive fireboxes and, because of the radical difference between the GWR and the other three of the 'Big Four', we will start there.

As a quick reminder of the facts, Welsh steam coal, as the name implies, is an excellent fuel for steam locomotives. However, because of its low volatile/high fixed carbon constituents, to burn it most effectively GW locomotives have certain design features. Being slow burning, a thicker firebed is needed, and because of the high fixed carbon content a higher ratio of primary to secondary air is required compared with the higher volatile matter locomotive coals. To this end, the air gaps between the firebars are greater and the blastpipe arrangements in the smokebox are designed to create a higher vacuum. In addition, the 4-6-0s with grates having the flat rear section and sloping front section have two additional dampers, front middle and rear middle, while the dampers themselves have only two positions: fully open or completely closed. These are the features that allowed 'haycock' fires to be used on services where steam demand could vary from low to extremely high.

It is a well known fact that G. J. Churchward combined best practice from around the world in the design of his standard classes, starting in the early 20th century. One aspect was the very high (for 1903) pressure of 225psi of the No 1 Boiler as fitted to the 'Saint' Class 4-6-0 express passenger and the '2800' Class 2-8-0 heavy freight engines, when other locomotive engineers seemed content with 180psi. Even 20 years later, the first Gresley 'Pacifics', including *Flying Scotsman* for example, still did not exceed 180psi. (The only other locomotive boilers in the 200 to 220psi range in the early 1900s were on the few compound engines built in that period, which needed a high pressure to provide the necessary differential between the high- and low-pressure cylinders.) As a result of that feature alone the Churchward engines were years ahead of their competitors.

As he was so meticulous in assessing all the information available before deciding which design features to incorporate, I am sure that he must have been aware that the greatest single influence on the efficiency of a steam locomotive was the performance of the man responsible for providing the power, i.e. the fireman, and that some used more than twice the amount of coal on the same duty as the best firemen did. The locomotives were so competent that they did not need to be pressed to anywhere near their maximum potential in order to keep time with the services, but consistency of firing performance was what was needed to improve overall thermal efficiency.

I am of the opinion that this was the thinking behind the haycock fire and the big shovel. The locomotive design features, in particular the two additional middle dampers, were such that very thick fires could be handled. Coal could be heaped up on the flat section of the grate in the vicinity of the join with the sloping section so that the angle of repose of the coal, combined with the oscillations of the locomotive, was sufficient to distribute the coal round the firebox. This meant that no great skill was required with the shovel and the coal did not have to

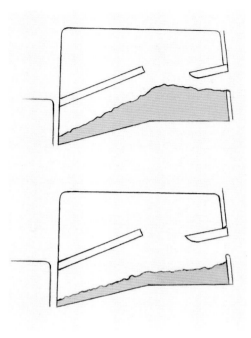

A 'haycock' fire of lowvolatile coal (above) compared with a thin fire of high volatile coal

be thrown far, so why not provide a big shovel that reduced the number of shovelfuls required on a journey by 50% and make the firemen happy?

Observant readers may have noticed on the illustrations of the GW firehole door arrangements a chain attached to the top of the flap. This is to allow it to be lowered and raised again after each shovelful of coal in order to reduce the cooling effect of excess secondary air entering the firebox when the doors are open. However, the flap has to be fairly thick and heavy in order to withstand the heat, and flicked up quite smartly so that the chain becomes slack just before the flap is fully raised in order to avoid it hitting the shelf over the firehole and causing the flap to drop back down. This requires a fair degree of physical effort on the part of the firemen, so it is not surprising that they soon began to build the fire well above the firehole ring, having discovered that the draught was sufficient to cope with very thick fires. This reduction in the effective area of the firehole was sufficient to preclude the need for the use of the flap between each shovelful, and the thick back on the fire meant much cooler conditions on the footplate when the flap was down. Some firemen took this to the extreme whereby only one shovelful of coal could be added at one time, which had to be pushed forward in order to make room for another one.

Thick firebeds of low volatile coal are slow to react to changes in smokebox vacuum – i.e. whether the regulator is open or closed, and hence the amount of primary air drawn through the grate. Very thick firebeds are very slow to react, so that a loss of pressure is likely to occur when sudden heavy demands for steam have to be made. However, the GW boilers could tolerate a drop of 40psi below the registered pressure and still provide pressures in excess of the maximum being used by other railway engineers. Likewise, by the time the regulator was closed, the fire would have heated up and been providing an excessive amount of steam. The combination of closing the dampers, opening the firehole door and using the injector(s), bearing in mind that the boiler pressure would normally be some way below maximum, should then have prevented blowing off.

The slow reaction time probably explains why the GW dampers were not fitted with arrangements for adjustable opening. When steam was needed, dampers had to be fully open, and when it was not the fire needed to be cooled as quickly as possible by shutting the dampers completely. The benefits of this are that combustion rates in the upper firebed are greatly reduced, due to the restricted oxygen supply. The cooling effects in the middle region are also reduced so that the temperature, if the delay is reasonably short, should still remain above the ash fusion temperature, thus avoiding the possible development of a deep bed of soft clinker.

The above method was clearly not the most efficient way to fire a locomotive, but it must have achieved a consistency of performance considerably higher than what would have been the average when firemen themselves decided which was the best or, more usually, the easiest way to fire. Churchward was therefore not only producing standard locomotives but also what amounted to a standard method of firing them, resulting in an overall improvement in thermal efficiency.

The use of the haycock fire was always a matter of great debate among the steam locomotive experts; one school of thought was of the opinion that GW locomotives performed well because of it, while conversely the other school was adamant that they did despite it.

With such thick fires, the maximum steaming capacity of boilers would normally never be reached, but in normal service this rate was rarely, if ever, required. What was more important was a good, consistent performance, and the haycock fire of low volatile coal almost guaranteed this.

Very thick fires, i.e. even thicker than what would be considered as a normal haycock fire, took a considerable time to build, so were only used on long-distance runs. A fireman taking over a locomotive on shed would have a reasonable depth of fire already prepared for him and he would no doubt start to thicken it before leaving the depot and while backing down onto the train. Making smoke in stations was frowned upon, but with the low volatile Welsh steam coal it was not a problem, so building up of the fire could continue. Coals have to be raised to a certain temperature, dependent upon the type being used, before they will ignite, and this is what was happening in the firebox.

Almost as soon as the train was under way, the fireman would insert the pricker into the firebox and close the doors so that the notch on each door, previously referred to, engaged with its shank. This provided a fulcrum and allowed the fireman to grasp the loop of the handle with both hands in order to pull the pricker at full depth of the blade through the heap of hot coal several times, exposing a lot more of its surface to oxidation. This reduced the resistance of the firebed, allowing more primary air to pass through and causing the top of the firebed to burst into flames. Welsh steam coals burn with a short flame as distinct from the high volatile long-flame coals.

With the fire now properly alight and the strong draught provided by the engine exhaust, the fireman could build up the fire to the level he desired. This meant quite hard work for a considerable time, but the fireman would be fresh and the benefit would come in the later stages of the journey when he would be more tired. Working on a regular route, with a heavy fire, a good fireman would know at what stage he could begin to run down the fire, and it is possible that the last 40 miles or so, on favourable gradients, might be covered with no more attention to the fire than an occasional livening up with the pricker from time to time.

As with all other types of coal, there are variations in Welsh steam coals. For example, the calorific value decreases from west to east across the South Wales coalfield, from the very low volatile anthracites of West Glamorgan to the relatively high volatile coals of East Monmouthshire, or Gwent as it is now called. Two other characteristics of Welsh steam coal that can also vary to a degree and occur in the firebox are caking and swelling. In some cases, in which the latter is most pronounced, the surface of the fire can become almost fluid.

The combination of caking and swelling normally results in some form of crust over the firebed, which is to some extent permeable to the rising hydrocarbons and still allows the fire to burn below it. I remember using one type of coal (probably one of the opencast coals) on which the crust was translucent with a gap between it and the firebed, which could be seen below. These crusts were brittle and all that was needed was a light rake over with the pricker from time to time to break them up and drop them onto the firebed.

So for main-line work on the GWR, the norm was to use heavy fires as distinct from the other railway companies of the 'Big Four' where wide varieties in locomotive coals and design features necessitated different firing methods in order to obtain best results. In order to help in achieving this, dampers were provided with devices to enable varying openings to be utilised, such as the LMS quadrant and lever type previously illustrated. British Railways took matters even further in its range of 'Standard' locomotives with screw-controlled damper doors allowing any adjustment between closed and fully open, but this type requires the fireman to estimate the damper opening from the length of thread on the damper control shaft protruding through the brass adjusting wheel, which is more difficult than checking which notch he is using on the shank or quadrant of the other types.

Whichever method of firing is used to meet the particular circumstances, the fireman should employ a firebed as thin as possible commensurate with the work required from the locomotive. How does the fireman know how thick this should be? Of course he doesn't until he has covered some distance so that he can get to know how the coal and the locomotive are performing. One thing for sure is that he must never start with what he considers to be the thinnest because, if he has misjudged it, the result may be having to stop for a blow-up. It is much more difficult to recover from dropping steam pressure and water level than it is to run the fire down a little in order to prevent blowing off.

There are a number of reasons for using the thinnest firebed, the most important, from an efficiency point of view, being quickness of response. The heat produced by a thin fire can be increased or reduced more quickly than a heavy one, which assists good boiler management. With a thin fire, the 'little and often' firing technique must be used, which not only reduces the amount of hydrocarbons given off at each firing, but also the time and degree to which the firehole doors are open. George Knight, the old Derby boilersmith, always insisted that the doors, in addition to their major role of adjusting the secondary air supply, were there to protect the crew from blow-backs or any other boiler problem that could discharge scalding steam and hot coals onto the footplate. Therefore the door opening at any time should be strictly limited to admitting the amount of secondary air required to consume the hydrocarbons. The damper controls should, of course, be adjusted in conjunction so that the hydrocarbons are not driven off the firebed more quickly than they can be burned.

Another very good reason is if the fire has to be dropped quickly due to a boiler problem. The primary objective is to protect the inner firebox while this takes place, so the injector(s) must be used to maintain an adequate water level. With conventional fixed grates, the fire has to be bailed out through the firehole, and a glance through that of a narrow-firebox engine will give some idea of the magnitude of this task. It is difficult enough with a fire that has not been run down enough prior to disposal. The GW-type tenders pre-Hawksworth, however, have distinct advantages in this task; firstly, the absence of a steel tender front and the lack of a shovelling plate means that, having loaded the clinker shovel, the fireman can back into the tender (sufficient coal having been used) and, secondly, drop the red-hot coals through an orifice below the firehole which is exposed by the removal of a steel plate that forms part of the footplate floor.

Unfortunately the business ends of the fire-irons get red hot and malleable very quickly and have to be quenched under the overflow from an injector by temporarily shutting off the steam supply to one if both injectors are being used to maintain the boiler water level. The shanks of the fire-irons also get very hot, so it is necessary to use thick hand cloths or protective gloves in order to avoid quite severe burns. The same applies to a lesser extent in cases where disposal takes place immediately after concluding a duty and the fire has not been adequately run down.

The use of a thin fire is also beneficial when out-of-course delays are encountered, because it cools down more quickly. I have read somewhere of firemen being advised to make a hole in the firebed to allow ingress of cool air to the firebox, but in my view it is best left undisturbed. With a reasonable depth of fire, if the damper is closed, the firedoors opened wide, the blower just cracked, the water level where it should be, and the injector used periodically to avoid blowing off, a considerable delay can be managed. Additionally, thin rounds of coal can be sprayed over the fire, which also has a cooling effect and has the benefit of providing coal in a state to flash up quickly and provide adequate steam for getting the train up to speed again.

If a long delay is envisaged, the fire can be blacked out. While waiting, the unburnt coal is being heated up towards its ignition temperature and, after starting away, two or three pulls-through with the pricker will quickly liven up the fire.

Some footplatemen propagate the myth that dampers should never be closed, as this results in clinker formation. This is clearly untrue, because clinker formation depends on the coal having a high enough ash content, the fusion temperature of which is exceeded by the firebed temperature when running, but then drops below it as the firebed descends onto the firebars and is cooled by the incoming primary air. With out-of-course delays, closing the damper as above reduces the rate at which the firebed cools and can prevent clinker formation provided the delay is not excessive (see later).

Hawksworth and Stanier tenders, because of the improved self-trimming design involving solid tender fronts with access doors, make dropping live fires on fixed grates extremely difficult and, I should imagine, virtually impossible. The introduction of rocking grates and hopper ashpans revolutionised the handling of this problem and I have no doubt that the incidence of damaged inner fireboxes was greatly reduced as a result of being able to dispose of the fire in a fraction of the time previously required. To dispel any thoughts that with current standards of locomotive and boiler maintenance such problems no longer exist, no fewer than three 'Pacifics' have been forced to drop their fires when running charter trains in recent years.

Running down fires for efficient disposal

I consider that it would be beneficial for all preserved locomotives other than small tank engines or 0-6-0s to be converted to rocking grates and hopper ashpans when undergoing overhaul, since the locomotives' appearance, so far as the general public is concerned, remains unaltered. In addition, it would greatly reduce the possibility of damage to the inner firebox in the event of a forced fire-drop, and lead to considerable benefits in the disposal process at the end of a long day.

With the Hawksworth and Stanier tenders, disposing of a partly run-down fire is difficult because the length of the fire-irons in a confined space makes manoeuvring them difficult. As a consequence heavy tongs are provided to enable firebars to be lifted out and the contents of the grate raked through the resultant gap between them. This sounds much easier than it is in practice.

If visiting an open day at a steam locomotive depot or works, look out for some firebars, which of course vary in length dependent on which type of grate they are to fit, and imagine the weight of the longer ones. Then remember that they have been under a fire burning large quantities of coal. Inevitably some fine ash gets into the narrow gap between the thickened sections at the ends and middle of the firebars, which are there to maintain the air gaps between them, and this causes additional friction when attempting to lift out the bars. This operation takes place in a grate containing some fire that is still at a pretty high temperature, and which could end in failure, resulting in a hot and sweaty crew now faced with paddling out the contents of the firebox. Due to the length of the paddle (clinker shovel), with Stanier tenders I found it less of a problem to tip the dead contents out through the side window, live fire must of course be dropped out of the door.

Back in the early 1970s on the SVR, unless the locomotive was in use the following day, in which case the fire was cleaned and a 'back' put on and banked down under the door, the instruction was to clear the grate. This provided the incentive for firemen to practise running down the fire on the last leg of a Sunday turn to provide an easier disposal. If the condition of the grate, as left, was not satisfactory, the offending crew would be hauled over the coals (pun intended). The challenge was to provide all the steam the driver wanted and, working off Bridgnorth, he usually wanted a fast run up the 1¾ miles of Eardington Bank, followed by barely a mile downhill from the summit to arrive at Bridgnorth with the minimum amount of fire in the box. Of course, with firemen anxious to provide sufficient steam for a storming run, this often resulted in rather more fire to be disposed of than was desirable.

This was all part of practising The Craft of the Fireman, and to illustrate how far it could be taken I shall refer to a firing turn with driver Ray Newey on LMS 'Black Five' No 45110, the locomotive that hauled the last leg of the famous 'Fifteen Guinea Special' on 11 August 1968, which brought steam haulage to an end on British Railways. As usual I put the injector on while I went to uncouple the stock after arrival at Bridgnorth. Access to the shed involves running forward on to Holly Bush Road siding and reversing through the free platform road to beyond the down home signal, followed by another reversal permitted by the calling-on signal to the shed yard. On the way round I noticed that the boiler pressure had fallen more quickly than I had anticipated, but I did not want to shut off the injector because they sometimes refuse to restart at low boiler pressure and the rule was to fill the boiler 'up to the whistle' if the locomotive was not in use the following day. This means out of sight above the gauge glass, the reason being that when locomotive boilers cool down there is a tendency for small leaks to open up. Filling boilers up to this level guaranteed that even if the locomotive was not lit up again for two or three weeks, there would be sufficient water in the boiler to do so.

On this particular occasion we rolled into the shed yard with the boiler full and only 60psi (registered pressure 225psi) on the gauge, so I applied the hand brake to be on the safe side. The firebars were showing on at least 50% of the flat section of the grate with dying embers on the rest and not much more on the inclined section. A perfect run-down? So far as disposal was concerned, yes, but perfectionists might argue that the boiler had been cooled down too quickly. However, a reduction from 225psi to 60psi would only mean about 80°F (44°C), and I certainly did not hear any bumps or bangs from the boiler that would have indicated too rapid a contraction.

Writing about this has reminded me of an occasion when running down the fire to a minimum caused a problem. It happened in 1981, by which time I had become a driver and was working off Bridgnorth for a week with the late Ken Quanborough firing, and it illustrates how things do not always go according to plan.

At that time the diagram was two round trips to Bewdley, then to Hampton Loade, where we changed trains. On Monday the Bewdley crew arrived with a huge fire in LMS Class 4MT 2-6-0 No 43106. It was obvious that no firing would be necessary, and even after arriving on shed the fire was still too big for a normal disposal; by normal I mean the fire in such a state that it allowed a proper inspection of the grate in order to carry out any necessary cleaning and leave a small fire banked down under the door overnight. Failure to do this with 70 miles to cover the following day before again changing locomotives would be asking for trouble, and a not very enjoyable day.

So, although reluctant to do so (at the time I was a director of SVR Holdings plc and well aware of the cost of coal), I decided to drop half of the fire, which was easy because of the rocking grate and hopper ashpan, thus enabling preparations for the following day to be done properly.

Ivatt 4MT 2-6-0 No 43106. *David C. Williams*

On Tuesday the Bewdley crew again arrived with a big fire, although not to the same excessive degree as on the Monday, so we asked them to reduce the size even further. As it happens they had experienced trouble with the rocking grate during disposal and failed No 43106, so on the Wednesday they arrived with No 7819 *Hinton Manor*. Ken had a look at the fire and asked me what I thought. I considered that even this smaller fire should be able to get us to Bridgnorth.

So off we set and about halfway up Eardington bank Ken had a look at the fire and said he thought he had better put a bit on, so I had a look myself and considered that there was enough to get us to the summit, from where it is only 1¼ miles (1.14km) into Bridgnorth, of which at least three-quarters of a mile (0.68km) is on a downhill gradient of 1 in 100. Even with steam off, trains accelerate on such a gradient.

Because we had a Great Western locomotive fitted with a vacuum pump, I did not bother to nurse the locomotive unduly in order to conserve steam, assuming that once over the summit, which we topped at 20mph at least, we should just coast down into Bridgnorth.

Unfortunately, the vacuum pump was obviously not performing as it should. I had reduced the steam pressure a bit too much so that the brakes must have been rubbing slightly, which gradually reduced the speed even further. Because the vacuum pump performance depends on the speed of the rotation of the driving wheels, it became even less effective and, with the remains of the fire cooling as well, steam pressure was slowly dropping so that the effect of the rubbing brakes gradually increased.

Even so, I thought we should still make it, but unfortunately there is a level section of track about 300 yards (275m) long south of the inner home signal, and we slowly came to a halt 10 yards (9.1m) from it, with the locomotive not much more than 100 yards (91.4m) from the end of the platform.

Fortunately, we were running about 5 minutes early and, even though there was not much fire left on the grate, the coal was good quality, of small size with high volatile matter and calorific value from Daw Mill. By carefully spraying small amounts over the remains of the fire, and judicious use of the blower, after about 10 minutes we managed to raise the steam pressure enough to release the brakes and get the train into the platform. With low volatile coals it is not advisable to run fires down to such fine margins, because of the much slower reaction rate.

This taught me a valuable lesson: never assume that anything on a steam locomotive is going to work as it should unless you have tested it. As the driver, I accepted responsibility, but I do consider that the delay was down to bad luck rather than bad judgement.

In the case of a locomotive in use the following day, the water level should be in sight near the top of the gauge glass, leaving sufficient room in the boiler to raise it to maximum pressure in order to check that the safety valves are operating within the prescribed limits, and be able to test both injectors while reducing the pressure to the desired amount.

However, this proved not to be the case on one occasion, in 1976 I think it was, when I was the rostered fireman for the Sunday service in the early days of the 'Santa Specials' running between Bewdley and Arley, when only one engine was required. At about 7.30 on the Saturday evening, the driver who had been on duty that day phoned me to tell me he had some bad news. This was to the effect that there was no water in the boiler (i.e. it was out of sight in the gauge glass) and no coal on the engine. To a fireman who had to prepare his engine in addition to working the turn, this was about the worst possible news. In my favour I knew that what water was still in the boiler would be quite hot and, as the engine was the WD 'Austerity' 0-6-0ST No 193 with a small boiler, it would not take long to raise steam once I had corrected the deficiencies.

Fortunately there was enough water in the saddle tank to provide a hydrostatic head sufficient to gravitate water into the boiler by blocking off an injector overflow and opening the appropriate valves. This saved me from having to remove a washout plug and insert a small-diameter hose. Having started this operation, I then carried bucketfuls of coal from the temporary stockpile by the goods shed – locomotives normally only being coaled at Bridgnorth – over to the engine standing on the inspection pit. By the time I had sufficient for lighting up I was able, by use of the test cocks, to bounce the water into sight at the bottom of the gauge glass and was thus able to proceed. Heating up the water also causes it to rise slightly in the glass. Forewarned was forearmed, and the first service left at the booked time.

16

Out on the road

To get back to firing and boiler management, other than the GW haycock
style of firing, there are just too many variables to be able to say what is
the correct way to fire. It all comes down to the individual fireman to decide,
from previous experience and trial and error on the day, what is the best way
to fire on that particular duty. In order to do this he must continually check
on steam pressure, boiler water level and the chimney top in order to make
adjustments to damper opening, firebed depth, secondary air and use of the
injector(s) against a background of the forthcoming demand for steam.

In going on to discuss deficiencies in firing on main-line charters I am not
intending any criticism. In effect, firemen of quite limited experience are taking
what, in steam days, would have been top link turns only earned after years of
progressing through the links. The running that we have had in recent years
and are still enjoying is far and away better than we are entitled to expect.
However, probably due to inexperience and lack of confidence, cases of boiler
mismanagement inevitably occur from time to time and, when discussing the
craft of the fireman, must be considered.

Any driver worth his salt will admit that becoming really proficient at the
art of firing takes years longer and requires more dedication and application
than that required for driving. I have come to the conclusion that drivers
were promoted to the top links as a reward for long reliable service rather
than exceptional driving skill. Indeed, the very top jobs, although high in
responsibility, mostly involved observing signals rather than adjusting the
locomotive controls.

Monitoring of the discharge from the chimney top gives a very good
indication of how efficiently the combustion process is being controlled and,
unfortunately, seems to be largely ignored by some firemen. I remember one
trip over Shap behind *Duchess of Sutherland*, back in 2005 I think it was, and
some sprightly running in the low 80s had taken place between Crewe and
Carnforth to the extent that we were all looking forward to a spirited run up
Grayrigg and Shap.

I was right at the back of the train and I began to get concerned by the
increasing amount of black smoke drifting away across the landscape. As I
anticipated, speed fell away too quickly on Shap and we eventually topped
the summit at a mediocre 24mph. Furthermore the chimney did not clear
completely until we approached the outskirts of Carlisle. It was pretty

LMS 'Pacific' No 46229 *Duchess of Hamilton. David C. Williams*

obvious that whoever was firing could not have been observing the fire or the chimney top and just kept baling the coal in, believing that this was what a 'Duchess' needed on Shap.

Some months later I alighted at Walsall from a Vintage Trains trip to Blackpool, hauled by *Kinlet Hall* if my memory serves me correctly. To my surprise the locomotive was, unusually, taking water and Bill Andrew was standing on the platform, so I went up to have a word. As usual we chatted about locomotive performance and I mentioned the trip behind the 'Duchess' and he told me that he took over the locomotive at Carlisle on that day (I was unaware of this as I had a tight connection to make after arrival back at Crewe) and the fire was still up to the brick arch, about which he was not very complimentary.

Black smoke can be caused for several reasons: either by blacking the fire out as above, so that the firebox temperature becomes too low to ignite the hydrocarbons, or introducing insufficient secondary air as a result of either putting too heavy a charge onto an incandescent fire at one firing, opening the damper too wide, closing the firehole doors too quickly, or a combination of all of these to a greater or lesser extent.

While on the subject of smoke, on more than one occasion a poor performance on the main line has been attributed to 'inferior coal' because of the amount of smoke produced. Instead of, 'There is no smoke without fire,' the fireman's adage is, or should be, 'There is no steam without smoke,' and the problems have probably been due to over-firing as in the case of the 'Duchess' above, or too much primary air/too little secondary air, wasting the valuable calorific value of the hydrocarbons. Of course, having created some smoke, it is incumbent upon the fireman to consume it so far as is possible. The exception to all this is a very low volatile Welsh steam coal, which is virtually smokeless.

Black smoke also causes soot deposits in the boiler tubes, which impair steaming, and if a fireman suspected that his locomotive was suffering as a result, it was not unknown for him to take a bucketful of sand – of which there was plenty available for the sandboxes – on board. When the locomotive was working hard, this could be sprayed off the shovel into the firebox and, due to its small size, it would go straight over the brick arch and through the boiler tubes. It was quite effective for tube cleaning, but due to its scouring effect on the firebox tubeplate and tubes, it was frowned upon by the authorities.

There also appears to be a popular misconception that GW engines are more selective than others with regard to types of coal, and will only perform properly with the best coals. I found the opposite to be true, and that the design features built into the GW locomotives for the burning of low volatile coals also makes them more effective in the combustion of lower-grade fuels.

I have previously indicated that it takes longer to alter the steaming rate with low volatile coals, and this is more pronounced on locomotives not designed to burn them because of their lower smokebox vacuum and narrower gap between the firebars. Consequently, it makes judgment of where and when to start building up the fire or running it down considerably more difficult, and GW engines can operate more efficiently on high volatile coals than other types on low volatile ones.

To achieve this means avoiding excessive black smoke and blowing off, so on GW engines with standard fittings it is necessary to provide some adjustment for the rear damper. This can be done by using two or three open-ended spanners of different lengths to sprag the damper control in the desired position. Failing this, different-sized blocks of wood can be used, which can be kept in the tender toolbox – or lumps of coal can be used.

A damper opening that is too wide when using high volatile coal is evidenced by blowing off against the regulator a short distance after starting from rest, sometimes for minutes at a time while the locomotive is still accelerating. Despite the relatively high steam demand, the boiler is producing steam at a rate higher than the locomotive is using it, because of the low speed. At the same time, the hydrocarbons are being driven off at a higher rate than the amount of secondary air provided by the fireman can consume them, resulting in black smoke. This is working a locomotive at its most inefficient, because coal is being wasted for two reasons: blowing off and wasting the calorific value of the unburnt hydrocarbons, in addition to the wastage of water.

Some crews also think that, because it is fitted, the flap should be used when firing GW locos, but with a high volatile coal and an incandescent fire, hydrocarbons are driven off very quickly after each shovelful, as evidenced by a puff of smoke at the chimney top. If the large GW shovel is being used, this is more pronounced and of longer duration, and raising the flap just at the time when extra secondary air is required is counter-productive.

Also to be avoided with high volatile coals is use of the middle dampers, particularly the front middle damper, with a normal tapering firebed – i.e. thicker at the back, thinner at the front. The front middle damper is very near the change from flat rear section to sloping front section of the grate underneath the thinnest depth of fire with a conventional firebed, and since primary air takes the path of least resistance, small pieces of coal can get ripped out of the firebed and carried through the tubes, rapidly filling the smokebox with char and causing steaming problems and the risk of a hole developing. The middle dampers are there to cope with the thickest part of haycock fires used with low volatile Welsh steam coal, and not to be used with high volatile coals and shallow fires.

A charter I travelled on that was beset with delays due to this cause was to Holyhead in 2006 with *Kinlet Hall*. Although I always take as much note as possible of the working of the locomotive, I do not presume to offer advice to footplate crews, but on this occasion I thought it would be helpful.

The run to the first water stop at Crewe had been enterprising, albeit to the accompaniment of some black smoke and blowing off. That the coal was of good quality and the locomotive steaming well was evidenced by the blowing off almost immediately on leaving, and the running then continued as before.

However, along the Dee estuary the running lost its sparkle, timings were missed and eventually we stopped at Abergele & Pensarn for what I suspected must be a blow-up. After about 7 minutes we restarted but with no great vigour, and ran quite slowly through Colwyn Bay, gradually slowing to a halt with the locomotive some distance short of the Llandudno Junction platforms, where we remained for a further 15 minutes before struggling in, 42 minutes down on our planned water stop arrival.

Before I could get anywhere near the locomotive it had been cordoned off and several wheelbarrows were being used to dispose of the smokebox char. By the time we left, the deficit had increased to 1 hour 12 minutes, but at least the delayed Holyhead services had been able to proceed.

With the smokebox emptied, the steaming capacity was restored, with plenty of black smoke and blowing off before we reached the estuary, and performance back to what it had been earlier in the day, but the delays to the service trains meant that we were held outside Holyhead until a platform became available. This resulted in the lateness increasing to 1 hour 51 minutes, and lunch – i.e. fish and chips – was overdue, so I left the station immediately.

When I returned the locomotive had just been coupled up to the train, so I asked the fireman what condition the smokebox was in on arrival. 'Full again,' he replied, so I said, 'What! After only 40 miles! How many dampers are you using?' My suspicions were confirmed when he said, 'Three.'

Although he was the relief fireman, I was aware that he had fired from Llandudno Junction, if not from Crewe. Because of the number of variables that can affect locomotive performance, it is customary for drivers and firemen to consult those they are relieving to establish whether or not there are any circumstances of which they should be aware. I can only conclude that the relief fireman was told that three dampers were required and blindly followed that advice with the inevitable result.

Now we had main-line experience with 'Halls' dating back to 1977 using the same type of high volatile cobbles, particularly on the Welsh Marches route between Newport and Chester, so I knew that on the relatively flat North Wales coast route the rear damper only, partly open by using one of the devices previously mentioned, would normally be sufficient.

As previously stated, using three dampers involves the middle dampers, the front one of which is sited under the point where the grate changes from level to inclined. With a conventional firebed this is normally the thinnest part of the fire, with the result that fairly large particles of coal are torn from the firebed when the locomotive is working, rapidly filling the smokebox.

When I told him one damper should be sufficient, he replied, 'No, you need three,' so I left him to it. The result was as before, the locomotive blowing off all the way up the steep climb out of Holyhead and intermittently, together with black smoke, crossing Anglesey.

I was not therefore unduly surprised when the locomotive was uncoupled from the train at the water stop at Llandudno Junction and run on to the loop where the smokebox was again emptied. This extended the water stop to 1 hour 1 minute and inevitably the locomotive blew off again as we left.

Before we arrived at Crewe an announcement was made over the PA system to the effect that passengers would have plenty of time to stretch their legs as the locomotive was out of coal and arrangements had been made for it to go on to the Heritage Centre to be coaled. This was not overly surprising, even though some coal had been taken on at Holyhead, bearing in mind that the smokebox had now been filled four times with unburnt char.

Slow running in the latter stages meant a 46-minute late arrival at Crewe, so with this further delay the train was now very late. Although I did not return to the point of origin, I believe arrival was almost 2 hours after the booked time.

Clearly on this occasion there was nothing wrong with the locomotive or the coal, but delays were caused to service trains, presumably incurring financial penalties, and it is not good for business to be 2 hours late getting home.

Instead of continuing to follow the advice given by the fireman, the relief fireman should have discovered that it was wrong and thought out how to correct the problem it had caused, thus reducing the consequences.

I will now give an example of a fireman causing himself some additional work and not apparently realising that he himself was responsible. On this occasion in 2008 I had been granted the privilege of a footplate ride on a BR 'Standard' Class 4 2-6-0 with a load of eight coaches on a fairly challenging route, the Cambrian Coast.

Unusually the fireman was using some front damper, so must have been of the opinion that the rear damper alone would be insufficient to meet steam demand.

With the firehole doors open and steam on, 'sparklers' were being projected from the firehole and landing on the footplate on average about 15 inches from the firehole, forming a conical pile, which, from time to time, he shovelled back into the firebox, then swept up.

More steam can, of course, be generated by use of the front damper, but the firebed must be thickened accordingly. In this case the firebed was too thin and particles within a certain size range were being ripped from the fire and accelerated under the brick arch to a velocity high enough to propel them back through the current of secondary air and out onto the footplate.

This must have caused the fire at the front of the grate to be cooler than desirable, so his use of the front damper was probably self-defeating and he would have raised the same quantity of steam by using the rear damper only. The outcome was to create for himself a small amount of additional work for no benefit.

It appears that many firemen tend to concentrate on the two most important aspects of boiler management – i.e. water level and pressure – and are satisfied if they manage to maintain these to the level required to meet the running schedules. To develop the craft of firing, it is necessary to observe all aspects and, if something out of the ordinary is occurring, to consider why and how to correct it.

Some high volatile coals have a swelling but non-caking property whereby particles of coal tend to split off the larger pieces and can get carried through into the smokebox in sufficient quantity to cause steaming problems. This can be alleviated if the fireman has closely observed the behaviour of the coal while the fire is in its early stages before it gets white hot and too dazzling to look at. A thicker fire is needed to reduce the rate of airflow through the firebed but still provide the same amount of heat as a result of the increase in the area of the coal surface exposed to oxidation.

No fireman, even though he has a reasonable knowledge of coal types and their appearance, can be sure that combustion and the results of it will always turn out as expected. For main-line running, because the watering facilities from steam days have been removed, it is usual to limit the distances between water stops to a maximum of about 70 miles, depending on capacity, in order to keep a reserve in the tender in case of excessive delays that do occur from time to time.

The fireman will know where, at what time, and for how long, the first water stop will be. It is not safe to assume that, just because there has not been any steaming problem en route, it will still be so after a water stop. The prudent fireman will run his fire down sufficiently to be able to check the condition of the grate by running the pricker over the bars. It may be that the coal has a relatively high ash content with a low fusion temperature, which leads to the formation of a soft clinker. When caught early, this breaks up easily and can be riddled through the bars into the ashpan.

All clinker starts in a molten form in the firebed, and as the firebed becomes lower due to the burning away of the fixed carbon and the oscillations of the locomotive causing ash to drop between the firebars, the cooling primary air reduces the temperature to below the ash fusion temperature, resulting in clinker on the bars. If the coal contains pyrites it becomes even more important to make an early inspection because any clinker will be of a hard metallic nature, which adheres to the firebars and the thicker it becomes the more difficult it is to break. With such coal a chisel bar should be carried in addition to the fire-irons already mentioned because the dart is not man enough to deal with a clinker akin to a furnace slag. This is simply a thick (1 inch or more) very heavy steel rod about 6 feet long with one end formed into a chisel blade and the normal loop handle at the other, which can be directed downwards with some force, assisted by its weight, into the clinker adhering to the bars.

Where and when to start running down the fire is of course purely a matter for the fireman's judgement, but if the well-known West Coast route from Crewe to Carlisle is taken as an example, and the fireman has a good fire on at Preston, he might well consider starting to run down the fire after accelerating back to speed following the Preston station slack. The distance to the normal water stop at Carnforth is only 26½ miles, and virtually flat, the last 6½ miles being mostly downhill, so boiler pressure could be allowed to drop by a considerable margin. With a high volatile coal it is easy to control the run-down because the coal flashes up very quickly, so if boiler pressure drops a little too fast it is only necessary to spray a few shovelfuls of coal occasionally across the top of the firebed in order to control the run-down to the desired rate.

While on the subject of running down fires, the top-class fireman always tries to judge as accurately as possible the point on the major climbs at which to start this process. Many of these are followed by lengthy downhill sections, and it is essential to have the fire reduced before passing the summit to avoid excessive blowing off on the descent. Often at the conclusion of a rousing climb, photographs show the locomotive blowing off, demonstrating that there has been no shortage of steam and captioned 'steam to spare'. In reality it is steam to waste, and a top-class fireman regards it as an affront to his boiler management skills.

When building up the fire again after checking/cleaning the grate, with the blower hard on and the damper fully open, steam can be raised quickly if coal is only added in small quantities, keeping the fire bright all the time. If even this is not fast enough, opening up the front damper and firing the front of the grate as well can speed up the rate to such an extent that the needle can sometimes be seen actually creeping round the scale. Fire cleaning such as this with limited time available is not possible with slow reacting low volatile coal.

I remember using this method on 'Black Five' No 5000 at Bewdley around 1981. The extension to Kidderminster had, at this time, not been made and our turn was due to finish there. Accordingly the fireman had run down the fire when, unexpectedly, we were asked to take over another train.

After coupling up, the fireman departed to replenish the tea supplies while I built up a new fire. As I was doing so, I noticed a fellow observing me from the platform, and when I put the shovel down he approached the footplate, saying, 'I see you can still get it down the front.' It turned out that he was an old Bushbury fireman who had fired the 'Jubilees' on the Wolverhampton-Euston services.

I wondered why he had used the word 'still', but then realised that he had been firing in the latter days of steam when, due to lack of recruitment as a result of full employment, most of the firemen were very young men. I think he assumed that I was the fireman, but I was 50 at the time.

The quality and calorific value of coal can vary considerably, and on occasion it is not up to the task of providing sufficient steam by normal firing methods. The only way to improve matters is by burning more coal per square foot of grate area, which can be achieved by use of the front damper. However, to do this successfully requires a 'back' to be built and maintained at the front of the grate, otherwise the fire will be lifted and a cool spot develop, thus defeating the objective.

With a sloping grate this is not difficult, but with a flat rear section it becomes tricky and requires a higher degree of skill to be effective. This is because the point where the level section of the grate meets the inclined section becomes the thinnest part of the firebed and, due to the amount of primary air entering the ash pan being greatly increased dependent on the degree of opening of the front damper, the fire will be lifted at this point unless adequately covered, again hampering the rate of steam production.

To avoid this, the fire must be kept thick here by building a hump in the firebed, but there is no great margin for error because if allowed to thicken much more than the minimum required it becomes impossible to fire the front adequately due to the proximity of the brick arch.

Insufficient coal will roll down to prevent the fire being lifted with the front damper open, again reducing the steaming rate, but the situation is easily remedied with the pricker by pushing the coal on the top of the hump forwards onto the inclined section.

The ideal situation before leaving a station from a cold start, or starting from an extended stop, is to have the blower on and the safety valves just about to lift at departure time with about three-quarters of a glass of water in the boiler. This enables the injector to be started to avoid any blowing off if there is a delay. The hot fire also means that the fireman can get everything under control more quickly after getting away.

To get back to the West Coast main line, leaving the down goods loop at Carnforth the gradient is slightly in favour for the first mile, but then follows 2 miles at 1 in 134 against, and another 3½ miles very slightly in favour before the start of the serious work on the climb to Grayrigg, which commences just before Milnthorpe and consists of 13 miles of adverse gradients culminating in 2 miles of 1 in 106. Then follows 5½ miles overall slightly in favour, and if the fire and boiler water levels are in the right condition this allows the driver to accelerate to the maximum authorised speed to attack Shap. In my view running down the fire has two benefits. Firstly, a clean grate gives the best prospects for steam generation for the hard work ahead, and secondly, on arrival at Carnforth, boiler pressure should be some way below maximum with a water level of half to three-quarters full, leaving plenty of room to allow the injector to be applied. Trains often arrive at Carnforth with too big a fire and the boiler almost full, so that regular blowing off occurs while taking water. The tendency then is for the fireman to overfill the boiler, and by that I mean to the top of the gauge glass, which is likely to result in an undesirable situation.

As an example I will quote an occasion some years back when Bill Andrew was in charge of *Duchess of Sutherland* (again) and the locomotive had been blowing off from time to time during the Carnforth water stop. We had left the loop and were not far into the 1 in 134 when the safety valves again lifted, so I anticipated what would happen next and was soon proved to be correct when the locomotive started to prime, i.e. water from the boiler was being carried over with the steam into the cylinders. As we have already seen, water is incompressible and damage to the motion (or even cylinder covers) can occur, so the driver must immediately open the drain cocks and close, or very considerably ease, the regulator dependent on the severity of the prime, which is something he would not wish to do on an adverse gradient.

Priming is normally caused either by the build-up of soluble salts in the boiler, which increase in concentration between boiler washouts, or carrying too high a water level. Main-line registered engines are no longer in continuous use and the maintenance schedules are such that cause number one is most unlikely. In the latter case if the boiler blows off, the surface of the water becomes extremely agitated to the extent that it gets carried over with the steam causing the prime. The quickest way to stop blowing off is to put the injector on, but if the boiler is already very full that is obviously undesirable. In the case of a heavy prime it is probably better to stop the train and allow the safety valves to reduce both pressure, stopping the blowing off, and water level if the train is on a steep gradient that requires heavy work by the locomotive.

However, if the driver is on top of his job and alert, he will be monitoring the chimney top and the sound of the locomotive. The whitening of the smoke or, in the case of a clear chimney, the appearance of steam round its rim together with a softening of the sharpness of the exhaust, will warn him that a prime has started. Under these circumstances, with the drain cocks open, reduced regulator opening, damper closed and firehole doors open to cool down the fire and stop the blowing off, the train can normally be kept moving. Bill must have caught it early because we certainly did not stop, but the last thing a locomotive wants when starting a period of heavy work is a prime of any degree, because the water, at a temperature that may be as high as 400°F (204°C), unfortunately washes the lubrication out of the valve chests and cylinders and, if sediment is also carried over, may reduce the effectiveness of the superheater.

As usual I went up to the locomotive after arrival at Carlisle and suggested to the crew that the boiler had been too full on leaving Carnforth and was told some cock-and-bull story as to why it had primed. At a later date Bill, to his credit, volunteered the information that I had been correct. Presumably he didn't want to embarrass his fireman.

I returned to the Citadel about half an hour before the booked departure time and saw to my dismay that the 'Duchess' was already blowing off intermittently with the relief crew on the footplate. The southbound climb to Shap commences almost immediately with 4 miles of 1 in 131. Guess what? The locomotive primed again after about half a mile.

With regard to excessive blowing off, South Wales and the South West have been the worst offenders in my experience. I particularly remember GW No 6024 *King Edward I* on the return leg of a 'Torbay Express' blowing off very noisily throughout a water stop at Taunton, and BR 'Standard' Class 'Pacific' No 70013 *Oliver Cromwell* for about 20 minutes after arrival at Bristol Temple Meads from a trip over the South Devon banks. The fire was clearly in a state to tackle Dainton at a time when the locomotive's work for the day was finished. These incidents must be very costly in terms of coal wasted.

I have since heard, but do not know whether or not it is true, that some senior jobsworth in the Western Region had specified that steam locomotive boilers must be kept up to maximum pressure when running. If so, he obviously knew nothing about operating steam locomotives.

Excessive blowing off results from big fires which themselves can have serious effects on running, as I discovered in September 1974. I was rostered for a Saturday afternoon relief turn from Bridgnorth, which I was able to cover by travelling straight from work. As the train arrived, the locomotive, LMS 'Jinty' 0-6-0T No 47383, was blowing off fit to burst and the fireman told me he had had trouble with steaming earlier in the day, but that there was no longer a problem. Well, there was obviously no problem with steam, but there was in the firebox, which was absolutely full of fire. There was nothing I could do, other than close the damper, open the firehole doors wide and top up the boiler from time to time, with the blower just cracked enough to keep hot gases from exuding into the cab.

This state of affairs continued virtually until just before departure time,

LMS 'Jinty' 0-6-0T No 47383. *David C. Williams*

when I put a quick round on the fire. The load was six coaches and the locomotive steamed reasonably well on the outward leg to Bewdley, but began to get more of a problem on the return trip. The locomotive was bunker-first in this direction and as it is only fitted with a front damper the pressure was not as high as I would have liked on Eardington Bank – the maximum is only 160psi anyway. During the afternoon Vaughan Welch, the driver, told me that the locomotive was diagrammed for an evening special and, so far as he knew, no fireman was covering it, so could I do it? Of course I agreed.

As the coal capacity of a 'Jinty' is only 2¼ tons, we had to go on shed to take coal and water and it was obvious that the fire needed to be looked at. By the time we had coaled and watered, the fire was well run down so we very quickly discovered that the whole grate was covered with a porous type of clinker resembling coke at least 12 inches (30cm) thick.

We set to in an attempt to clear the grate but, although relatively soft, the clinker was so thick that it was very difficult to break through. Having hacked some pieces off the surface, we eventually managed to excavate a huge chunk out of the middle of it. By huge I do mean *huge*, like a big football, and we only got it through the firehole, 18 inches (45cm) in diameter, by hooking the pricker round behind it to keep it on the shovel. All that was left of the fire was a few blue flames licking round the sides of the box, and as departure time was looming it was time to try and get some sort of fire going. At least we had the benefit of a high volatile coal (Granville cobbles, I think), which flashed up quickly.

When a locomotive is on the move, clinker only forms on the grate because the firebed above it is hot enough to keep ash molten in cases where the ash fusion temperature is low enough for it to melt. In our case, because the loco was stationary, a deep firebed had cooled to a temperature below the ash fusion temperature and, as the coal also contained some pyrites, a slightly porous, slightly metallic, deep bed of clinker had formed.

The diagram for the evening working was empty coaching stock (e.c.s.) Bridgnorth to Arley, passenger Arley to Bewdley, Bewdley to Bridgnorth, Bridgnorth to Arley, and e.c.s. from Arley to Bewdley and Bridgnorth. This was necessary because at this stage the loop at Arley had not been reinstated. So another 50 train miles was involved, and with the grate in such a condition it was not going to be easy.

I was pleasantly surprised by the performance of the fire and we did not have a problem with the adverse gradients out of Arley, Highley and Hampton Loade on the first return leg as we were running non-stop, but Eardington Bank is a different kettle of fish, and by this time a very strong draught had developed through the firehole. This resulted in a firework display from the chimney and some red-hot particles about half the size of a golf ball were being ejected high into the air and bouncing off the roof of the second coach about a quarter of the way along its length. I have no idea what the passengers thought might be happening.

Anyway, we got them back to Arley, then ran e.c.s. to Bewdley where the signalman, typical of Bewdley, asked us to do a shunt for him as we ran round, although it was now about 11.30pm. As you can imagine, by now the condition of the fire had worsened and on the return from Bewdley the draught through the firehole was such that the shovel only had to be presented somewhere near the firehole protection ring and the coal would be sucked off it. This was not very productive since it resulted in a lot of it, as we were now down to fairly small stuff in the corners of the bunker because of our heavy coal consumption, going straight over the brick arch through the tubes and out of the chimney. So I resorted to completely inverting the shovel blade as it passed through the firehole and directing as much of the coal as possible downwards onto the top of the fire, which was almost up to the level of the firehole. I did learn an important lesson: because the tremendous draught almost snatched the shovel out of my hands on one occasion, I always carried a spare. Without one you can find yourself up the creek without a paddle (other than the clinker paddle, which is impossible to fire with!).

We eventually arrived back on shed at Bridgnorth at about 12.30am expecting an arduous disposal, and we were both tired. Vaughan had been with the engine since around 7.30am on Saturday and I had been at the colliery at the same time. To our great relief we were rescued by two Good Samaritans in the shape of Dave Reynolds and Derek Tuck, who not only took over the disposal but also provided us with free fish and chips. Talk about good mates!

Now my wife would have been expecting me home at about 8.30pm or so on Saturday because I only knew about the evening turn late on Saturday afternoon. The problems with the engine had prevented me from phoning from Bridgnorth and it was 2.00am when I arrived home. So as not to disturb her, I let myself in quietly and was just creeping across the hall when Fay's voice came from the landing: 'You're not going to tell me that you run trains till this time of night?' So you see, even the harmless pursuit of firing steam engines can sometimes get you into trouble.

The reason for recounting the above is because of an incident that occurred on a main-line charter in about 1996, involving a big fire and excessive blowing off with BR 'Standard' Class 7 'Pacific' No 70000 *Britannia*. We had had a very spirited and enjoyable run back from Swansea and stopped at Platform 1 at Newport to take water en route to Gloucester.

On this occasion Fay was with me and as it was after dark on a not very pleasant evening, I did not bother to get off and go up to the engine. However, the engine was blowing off heavily when we arrived and had continued to do so for about 10 minutes, so I decided to go and have a look. The engine was still blowing its head off, there was no one on the footplate and nobody appeared to be taking any notice, so I got back on the train.

We set off without much vigour from Newport and hadn't got very far past Llanwern when we slowed to a stop. As no normal brake application had been made, nor any announcement as to the reason for the delay, one of the keen travellers went off to investigate and came back saying, 'The engine's down the pan.'

The problem was a clinkered fire and my mind went back to the 1974 incident just described; I was pretty sure that the same type of clinker had formed. The fire must have been in such a dead state that some cleaning could take place and we eventually got under way again, but some very slow running

BR 'Standard' Class 7 'Pacific' No 70000 *Britannia. David C. Williams*

to Gloucester meant a rather late arrival. Out-of-course stops followed by slow running almost inevitably mean delays to service trains, resulting in penalty charges. Such occurrences must therefore be avoided.

Practising a craft over a period of time, while not perfecting it, instils a skill and discipline that remains after such practice has ceased, as a final anecdote of my own experience shows.

I was at Bridgnorth station on 6 August 2008 when the train from Kidderminster arrived, headed by none other than 'Black Five' No 45110, a historic locomotive in its own right, and one that I had fired under supervision for the first time on Easter Sunday 1974. A boiler certificate extension had been granted to allow it to haul its final train on 11 August before withdrawal for heavy overhaul, this being the 40th anniversary of it heading the last steam-hauled train operated by British Railways.

As I knew both driver Fred Cotterell and fireman Bob Heath well, I approached the locomotive to have the usual chat and was invited to join them in running the locomotive round the train. This was the first time I had been on the footplate of a moving steam locomotive since 1994, when I had stepped down due to the impact of very heavy personal commitments.

Later on the same day it struck me that I might not ever see No 45110 in steam again, as the wait for it to enter Bridgnorth works would be considerable. I thought that it would be very nice if I could make a footplate trip on it before its withdrawal within the week, so I contacted Fred with such a request, and he very kindly agreed and said he would arrange it for the following day at the same time.

Next morning I retrieved my boots, overalls and greasetop from the garage loft so that I could present myself at the locomotive properly attired. Bob said that I could make the fire up and fire the locomotive as far as I wanted, which I was very happy to do. Then I looked at the coal for the first time and was amazed to see that it contained a fair proportion of large lumps instead of the usual cobbles. This should of course be broken into pieces about the size of a man's fist, i.e. cobble size, but I decided to accept the challenge of firing with the coal as it was; this, of course, makes boiler management more difficult because of the slower response of the fire at times of increased steam demand, due to the decreased area of coal available for oxidation. In saying large lumps, I do mean *large*, as the biggest was up to the size of the pan of the shovel itself.

The 1 in 100 gradient to Eardington summit actually starts within the platform length and continues for about a mile, so this would be the most difficult section in which to keep boiler pressure within 10psi of blowing off, bearing in mind a relatively cold start after the layover. However, things went well as Bob observed, 'You've got a good fire on,' with the needle steady on 215psi approaching the tunnel and the climb was achieved without dropping more than 10psi below the registered pressure.

A slight blemish occurred approaching Arley. I was a bit late setting the injector, which then blew out on braking ready for the station stop and a

The author, aged 76, at Bridgnorth on 7 August 2008, having fired the 11.55am to Kidderminster and driven the 2.00pm return. *Fred Cotterell*

safety valve lifted very briefly before I could reset it.

At Bewdley I made up the fire for the climb to Foley Park Tunnel and filled the boiler to between three-quarters and full, knowing that this would be sufficient to obviate use of the injector on the climb. As we were running tender-first, even if the water was in the bottom of the glass at the summit none would be needed due to the change of gradient increasing the depth of water over the firebox crown plate. The needle was steady on 220psi up the bank and through the tunnel, so I set the injector just before the summit and on arrival at Kidderminster the pressure was down to 200psi with enough room left in the boiler. I then opened the firehole doors for the first time since leaving Bewdley and was most gratified to see a perfect uniformly dull red firebed. I could hardly believe it. We were able to leave the locomotive and go to have a bite of lunch in the full knowledge that it would behave itself until our return.

So, with a bit of luck, I still almost managed to achieve a firing trip within the parameters I first set back in the early 1970s. To cap a most enjoyable day Fred also granted me the privilege of driving the train back to Bridgnorth.

17

Conclusion

The ultimate objective of a craftsman is perfection, and I hope that I have illustrated how difficult that is to achieve in the case of firing a steam locomotive. I have not intended to be overly critical of some firing performances, but it has been necessary to explain what can go wrong when they fall below the required standards; indeed, I am full of admiration and extremely grateful for the many thousands of miles of fine running and countless hours of enjoyment they have provided me with over the years.

I particularly enjoy locomotives tackling long gradients at speed, especially when I am close to the engine, the thrilling exhaust of which demonstrates the immense power being exerted. I never cease to be amazed by the enormous quantities of steam generated by the firemen to enable these exciting climbs to be achieved.

Anyone who has been on the footplate of a stationary locomotive in steam might be misled by its quiescent state, which is so different from that of one in serious action. R. F. Hanks, Chairman of the Western Region of BR, in his speech at the naming ceremony at Swindon in March 1960 of BR Class 9 No 92220 *Evening Star*, the last steam locomotive built for British Railways, effectively said as much: 'No other machine, somehow, is so human and so gentle yet, when unleashed, is capable of such noble power and strength.'

In these days when human physical effort has largely been supplanted by mechanical means, that required to fire a big engine for 250 miles or more with 400 or 500 tons on the drawbar must rank very highly. That this has to be done under conditions far from conducive was well summarised by Professor W. A. Tuplin, who wrote, '…but remember that steam power was maintained by the toil of a man on the writhing connection between the two roughest riding vehicles of the whole train. From hard labour in the fireman's tumultuous kingdom, came the power and the glory for ever and ever preserved in train timers' logs for resurrection, re-assessment and re-admiration.'

No one, not even the driver, can assess how well the fireman has done his job. The driver does, of course, glance from time to time at the boiler water and pressure gauges, but will concentrate mainly on observing signals and the line ahead while working the locomotive.

As far as the passengers are concerned, those interested in locomotive performance might take notice of the colour of the smoke and, if close enough, whether the engine is blowing off. Only the fireman himself will know to what extent he has made dark smoke, allowed the boiler to blow off or how closely to the registered value he has managed to maintain the pressure, so why bother?

The answer is that to a fireman attempting to perfect the art of firing, pride in performance and job satisfaction mean everything.

So the next time you travel behind steam and perhaps go up to admire the locomotive after arrival, at the same time look at the length of the train and imagine the power that has been required to complete the journey. Try to identify the fireman and look at him through a new pair of eyes. Give him the respect and accolade that he deserves. Without his skill and stamina, none of what has just taken place would have been possible.

Notes

Notes

Notes